SKILL-BUILDING
FOR SELF-DIRECTED
TEAM MEMBERS

Successful Self-Directed Work Teams don't just happen — success depends on training Team Members!

This book/workbook was designed to help SDWT, TQM Team Members and other Employee Involvement Team Members develop the critical skills they need. It can be used by the Team Leader or Team Member alone—reading at his/her own pace and answering the questions. It also has exercises for the entire Team to do together and build a stronger, more effective, more productive Team!

SDWTs aren't effective overnight. They evolve through the training and development of all the members.

For: Team Members
Team Leaders / Facilitators
Coordinators / Managers
Trainers

Contains: Readings, Exercises, Checklists, Assessments, And More!

i

Skill-Building for Self-Directed Team Members
By Ann & Bob Harper

Printed and bound in the United States of America
Library of Congress Card # 91-90570
ISBN: 1-880859-02-5

To order additional copies, call MW Corporation at 914-528-0888.
Quantity discounts available. See Chapter 20 of this book for
information on this and other books, videos, and training.

SPECIAL THANKS
To MW Corporation Associates
for all their help and support.

Our Purpose

A group of people working together is not necessarily a Team. Building the Team Member's skills makes the difference.

This book was written for people who belong to, lead, facilitate, or support Teams. We designed it to contain the critical skills work team members need in order to be effective. The information comes from our own experience in working with Team Members, so we know it's effective.

Our aim is to:

■ Build your skills in: Communication, Customer Service, Continuous Improvement, Change Management, Motivation, Group Dynamics, Team Meetings, Decision-making, Problem-solving, Leadership/Membership, Listening, Giving & Receiving Feedback, Managing Conflict, etc.

■ Help you understand why Teams are essential to competitiveness.

■ Explain how much you and the organization have to gain from Self-Direction.

■ Show you why SDWTs not only work, they make sense!

■ Help your Team develop self-directed skills (even if you're a Quality Improvement Team, Project Team, CI Team, EI Team, etc.)

■ Get you excited about the opportunities for improved Quality, Productivity, Job Satisfaction, Performance, and Reward that Teams can provide.

■ Increase your awareness that what you do and think makes all the difference. That you have the power to work smarter, more creatively, and compete successfully with any worker, anywhere in the world in creating the best product or service with the highest quality!

■ Help you become a member of the best Team ever!

This Book
Belongs To:

_____

Questions This Book Will Address:

We've been asking people in our training sessions to tell us what questions they'd like addressed. This book is partly the result of listening and answering those questions.

1. What is a self-directed, self-managing, high-performing team?

2. Why is teamwork more important than it used to be?

3. What evidence is there that teams can perform better than individuals?

4. What attitudes and skills are necessary for an effective team member?

5. Can anyone learn to be an effective team member?

6. Will I have to give up my individuality in order to belong to a team?

7. What do I do when conflict occurs?

8. How can a team make an effective decision?

9. Can a team solve a problem better than any one individual?

10. What is "continuous improvement?"

11. What are the stages of development a group goes through?

12. What do you do if your group gets stalled and can't seem to progress?

13. What do I do if I don't trust the members of my group?

14. What kind of training does a self-directed work team need?

15. What kind of leadership does a team need? (Does a SDWT need a leader?)

16. What do I do when it's my turn to be leader?

17. What do we need to do to conduct an effective team meeting that accomplishes things and is not a waste of time?

18. Which companies have SDWTs?

19. What systems need to change in order to have SDWTS—Appraisal? Rewards?

20. What is an internal customer?

21. How do I know if my team is effective? And how can I help it keep improving?

22. What are the group dynamics I can expect?

23. What does empowerment really mean?

24. How can I improve my communication skills?

25. How important is listening to this new way of working?

26. How can I give and get feedback without alienating people?

27. How do I make sure my team gets the support it needs?

28. What motivates me? What motivates other people?

29. What is the best decision-making style?

30. Is everyone creative?

31. Is this employee involvement movement just another "program" or is it really a permanent change?

32. How do you teach adults?

33. Can you measure team effectiveness? How? What?

34. What does it mean to be customer-driven?

35. How long does this process take from start-up to maturity?

36. Is there a "best way" to develop SDWTs?

37. How important is top-management commitment?

38. How can you tell if management is really committed?

39. Is this a Japanese idea and doesn't it only work in their culture?

40. How important are rewards?

41. Which companies are using profit-sharing, gainsharing, pay-for-knowledge, pay-for-skills, etc.?

42. Are self-directed work teams only possible in manufacturing settings? What are the service examples?

43. How important is it that the team leader, supervisor, manager—change their role?

44. Is it possible to have a "leaderless team?"

45. What do you do with a "difficult" team member?

Table of Contents:

The following chapters do not have to be read or used in consecutive order. They were created to be examples of "self-directed learning." Each chapter stands alone so the reader can choose the order that is best for him/her.

Page

Introduction ix

Chapter 1: *Why Success In Today's Organization Depends on Teamwork* 1
Reasons Self-Directed Teams Work • The New Economic Realities
• American Success Stories-Model Companies • Questions

Chapter 2: *Characteristics of Successful Self-Directed Work Teams* 9
Definition of SDWTs • Questions • How SDWTs Are Different from
Traditional Work • Design & Implementation of SDWTs • Important
Redesign Considerations • Questions

Chapter 3: *How "Teams" Are Different From Groups* 21
Individual Exercise on Best Team Experience • 10 Key Traits of Successful
Teams • Team-Building Assessment • Team Exercise • Guidelines for
Brainstorming

Chapter 4: *Setting Team Ground Rules & Examining Norms* 33
Individual Exercise on Assumptions About Teams • Team Consensus
Exercise • Guidelines for Reaching Consensus • The Purpose of Team
Ground Rules • Team Exercise on Establishing Ground Rules
• Team Exercise on Examining "Norms" • Questions

Chapter 5: *Characteristics of The Effective Team Member* 43
Self-Assessment: How Do You Rate As A Team Member? • Action
Commitments • Team Exercise

Chapter 6: *Measuring Your Team* 49
Assessments for Determining How Self-Directed Your Team Is Now on
3 Dimensions: Operational Tasks/Responsibilities, Administrative Tasks/
Responsibilities, and Training Received • Team Exercise • Measuring &
Evaluating How the Team is Doing • Peer Assessments • Questions

Chapter 7: *The Role of the Team Leader* 59
Individual Exercise on Leadership • Team Exercise • Qualities of
Effective Leaders • New Leadership Skills Needed • SDWT Leadership
Assessment • Questions • How the Leadership Role is Different
in SDWT Environment Vs. the Traditional Organizational Model
• A New View of Leadership • Skills, Attitudes, & Beliefs of
Effective Team Leaders • "Shared" Team Leadership - Benefits
• Leadership Self-Assessment • Action Commitments

Chapter 8: *Stages of SDW Team Development* 73
What to Expect, What to Do, & Training Needed at Each of the 3 Stages
of SDWT Development • Management's New Role • Questions
• How to Keep Your Team Developing • Team Exercise
• Action Commitments

Chapter 9: *Effective Team Meetings* 85
Importance of Team Meetings • Team Meeting Assessment
• Team Exercise • Action Commitments

Chapter 10: *Communication: Listening & Sharing Information* 93
Listening Questionnaire • Why Listening Is The #1 Skill of An Effective
Team Member • Definition of "Active" Listening • Listening & Facilitation
• Listening & Values • Team Paraphrasing Exercise • Self-Assessment
• Questions • Action Commitments • Information-Sharing: Disclosure
• Team Exercise • Feedback Sharing • Team Exercise

Chapter 11: *Understanding Group Dynamics* 109
Group Dynamics Assessment • Actions to Facilitate Positive Dynamics
• Team Climate Survey • Discussion • Action Commitments

Chapter 12: *Decision-Making* 119
Team Decision-Making Exercise • "Process" Assessment • Conditions for
Synergy • Team Exercise • 3 Decision-making Styles • Empowerment
• Criteria for a "Good" Decision • Kinds of Decisions SDWTs Make
• Empowering Teams • Team Exercise

Chapter 13: *Managing Conflict* 131
Conflict Management Team Exercise • Questions • Determining Your
Conflict Style: Individual Exercise • 3 Conflict Styles
• Action Commitments • Team Exercise on Setting Ground Rules for Conflict

Chapter 14: *Motivation & Rewards (Intrinsic & Extrinsic)* 145
Individual Exercise on Motivation Assumptions • Team Consensus
Exercise • 26 Key Points About Motivation • Needs Theory
• Importance of Reward Systems • Compensation Systems That Work
• Profit-Sharing, Gainsharing, Bonuses, Pay-for-Skills, & Pay-for-Knowledge
• What Is Needed To Make Incentive Plans Effective • Company Examples
• Team Exercise

Chapter 15: *Facilitating The Adult Learner* 159
Critical Needs for Successful Adult Learning • Role of the Facilitator:
Skills Needed

Chapter 16: *Managing Change* 165
State-of-Mind Shift • Shape of the Successful Organization • Coping
With the 4 Stages of Change • Overcoming Barriers to Change • Questions

Chapter 17: *Quality Customer Service* 175
Customer Service Research • Questions • Team Exercise on Improving
Customer Service • Steps in the Service Cycle • Action Commitments

Chapter 18: *Problem-Solving for Continuous Improvement* 185
Defining Continuous Improvement • Questions on How You Do Things
Now • Rating Yourself As Your Customers Would • Relationships with
Vendors, Suppliers, Support Groups • Examining the Team's Work
Processes • Team Exercise: 7-Step Problem Solving

Chapter 19: *For Further Reading - A Bibliography* 209

Chapter 20: *Products & Services to Support SDWTs* 213

Introduction

As we move towards the 21st century the creation, leadership and development of HIGH-PERFORMING TEAMS (whether they are called self-directing, self-managing, high-involvement, etc.) is a major issue. Companies that have informed, motivated, skilled, trained, and committed people will out-perform companies that still operate in the traditional way. It's that simple and critical that narrow, isolated jobs give way to the creation of whole tasks (products or services) executed by high-performing teams.

In our first book, *SUCCEEDING AS A SELF-DIRECTED WORK TEAM: 20 Important Questions Answered,* we described what SDWTs were, why they are critical now, how to design and implement them, etc. Once an organization has SDWTs the critical task is to develop the team members and the team as a whole. That is the purpose of this book: To help Team Members develop their skills individually and as a Team.

The Skills We Will Address Are:

- Communication
  - Listening
  - Feedback
  - Information Sharing
- Continuous Improvement
- Customer Service
- Managing Change
- Motivation - (Understanding Yourself & Others)
- Handling Conflict
- Using Diversity As An Asset
- Team Development
- Group Dynamics
- Decision-making
- Problem-solving

- Synergy & Creativity
- Understanding the Stages of SDWT Development
- Team Leadership
- Team Membership
- Self-Assessment
- Team Assessment
- Adult Learning
- Measurement & Rewards
- Positive Feedback
- Effective Team Meetings
- Setting Team Norms
- Facilitating Teams
- Employee Involvement Skills
- Self-Direction Skills

Chapter 1

Why Success in Today's Organization Depends on Teamwork

The reasons Self-Directed Teams work and some examples of successful American companies that have them

Why Success in Today's Organization Depends on Teamwork 1

Despite all the change and upheaval in American companies lately the one thing everyone agrees on is that we are in a new economic age where the rules of the game as it used to be played no longer work. So, we have to learn to play a new game and almost always this involves forming and maintaining high-performing teams.

Whether we call these teams self-directed, self-managed, quality improvement, employee involvement, high-involvement work teams, or something else, their purpose is always the same: to help us compete in the global marketplace by working smarter. Smart systems, empowered workers, and incredible teamwork are needed by all organizations regardless of whether you are in manufacturing or service, union, or non-union, profit or non-profit settings.

Let's look at the new economic realities and why High-Performing Teams are best suited to competing during these times:

1. High-Performing Teams Can React Quickly to Change

Nothing is stable and predictable anymore so we need to be able to respond quickly to change whether it's driven by a customer, or by changes in the market, or anything else. The traditional, bureaucratic, slow-moving organization cannot compete with the faster, more nimble one. After all the reorganization that has taken place within American auto companies, some are still reducing as many as 17 and 21 layers in order to better compete with Toyota that only has seven. The winners will produce more cars with higher quality in less time by staying flat, lean, flexible and fast.

2. High-Performing Teams Can Deliver Higher Quality and Better Customer Service

For a very long time American industry inspected for quality instead of concentrating on building it into products and services. Not only was this wasteful but it underutilized our workers. Companies are finding that teams of multi-skilled workers organized around producing a product or delivering a service can eliminate mistakes and deliver better quality and service to customers—who after all determine what quality is. By reorganizing into teams, American Express was able to cut their 30-day cycle for replacing a lost or stolen credit card to 24 hours!

3. High-Performing Teams Can Constantly Improve Everything

The Japanese call it KAIZEN: the constant improvement of everything by everyone. The attitude is one of, "If it's not perfect, improve it." Do something every day to make something better. We're learning that companies that institute constant improvement and reward it, reap benefits in terms of customer satisfaction, worker satisfaction, money

3

saved, costs lowered, cycles shortened, excessive bureaucracy eliminated, etc. Team Xerox has since 1983 returned the company to dominance in the copier market by turning everyone's focus to quality as defined by the customer. Xerox has won a Malcolm Baldrige award for quality.

4. High-Performing Teams Improve The Motivation, Satisfaction and Productivity of Workers

Only motivated, committed workers can successfully compete in the global marketplace. Working smarter can only be achieved with an involved workforce. Teamwork can fulfill needs in workers that enhance motivation, job-satisfaction and, ultimately, productivity.

Johnsonville Sausage's Pride Teams have helped the company increase its share of the sausage market in greater Milwaukee from 7% in 1978 to 46% today. Recently, according to Training Magazine, the workers at Johnsonville decided to work 7-days a week for a

period of time to take on a new customer. Workers, here, also share in the profits and everyone gains.

5. High-Performing Teams Can Constantly Learn, Self-Correct, And Respond To Opportunities

Only the organization that constantly trains and retrains its people will succeed. In this fast-changing world skills become obsolete very quickly so constant updating of technical knowledge is critical and so too are skills for effective team membership — communication, problem-solving, etc. As people constantly learn and teams examine how they operate and self-correct for improvements, they can respond to opportunities.

At Quad Graphics (high quality magazine printers who most years win Newsweek's award for best quality) workers, organized into teams, train a half-day a week every week on their own time. No one ever graduates from Quad Tech because they're always adding new courses.

American Success Stories in Union and Non-Union Settings

Here are more examples of companies that have used HIGH-PERFORMING TEAMS to speed processes, shorten cycles, improve customer service, improve quality, improve everything constantly, train and retrain, and thus be able to seize opportunities that would have been impossible otherwise. Lest you think this is not possible in union environments, the following examples come from the U.S. Dept. of Labor and reflect the results of union and management partnerships.

ROHM AND HAAS - LOUISVILLE, KY
Began in 1985 to redesign the workplace for 640 employees. The work teams that produce plastic and chemical products

have increased worker motivation and a sense of ownership in the company as a whole. Success is measured through a decrease in grievances, improved safety performance, a decrease in customer complaints, and an increase in productivity. Quality has improved, and because teams are allowed more flexibility to implement product improvement changes, absenteeism and turnover have also been reduced. Rohm and Haas has an annual Quality of Work Life Conference with delegates from all plants throughout the U.S.

GE PLASTICS; BORG-WARNER CHEMICAL, INC. BAYMAR PLANT, ST. LOUIS, MO.

Beginning in 1982, 81 technicians organized into work teams solve problems by consensus, and make decisions on how best to operate. Team members are cross-trained and rotate through various jobs. Hiring and resolution of personnel problems are also handled by the teams. Accomplishments include decreases in injuries, increased capacity, improved quality of work environment, and higher employee morale.

SHENENDOAH LIFE INSURANCE COMPANY - ROANOKE, VA

Eight self-managing work teams with 6-10 members each were implemented in 1983 after a socio-technical analysis of certain operations indicated that the work could be better structured. By eliminating functions the teams are able to be more efficient and streamlined. This has resulted in work volume increasing while the number of workers needed to do the work has decreased. The supervisor/employee ratio has been reduced from 1:7 to 1:37 (there are no supervisors, the teams report directly to a general manager who has responsibility for 45 people), and the number of complaints from customers has decreased dramatically. Within the teams, the group rather than the individuals are held accountable. Team members are

paid for learning. They receive a base salary with increments for each new skill acquired. Peers determine whether an individual team member merits a work skill pay increase. Management determines how the team is doing in terms of hiring, training, disciplining, etc.

NUMMI (New United Motor Manufacturing, Inc.) FREMONT, CA

A joint venture between Toyota, General Motors, and the UAW has produced astonishing results. Starting in 1984 with a facility that had a history of hostile union/labor relations and poor product quality, this plant has been turned around into a producer with some of the highest quality GM products, low absenteeism, and a high-level of trust between the union and management. 2,500 people are organized into self-directed work teams of 4-6 people. Each team has a Team Leader who reports to a Group Leader. Each team meets regularly to coordinate the team's effort but does not discipline. A suggestion system makes it possible for any employee to submit a suggestion on productivity or improvement of the work environment. Teams decide on policy, personnel, and procedures. Training is on-going.

A recent survey by the Productivity Quality Center in Houston of 476 Fortune 1,000 companies showed that while only 7% of the workforce is now organized into self-directed work teams, half the companies interviewed said they planned to have them.

Two years ago **Federal Express** organized 1,000 clerical workers into self-managing teams. The company feels these teams contributed to the 13% improvement in preventing lost packages, producing correct bills, and other service improvements. One of these teams recently saved the company $2.1 million by coming up with an idea (during their team meetings) to correct a billing problem. (Fortune Magazine, May 1990)

In 1989 Business Week described teams at GE and AT & T in an article entitled, "The Payoff From Teamwork."

A **GE** plant in Salisbury, NC is able to produce customized lighting panel boards with teams of flexible workers who can move from job-to-job because they are cross-trained. This enables them to respond quickly to customers who have special needs for customized products. GE reports that this plant is 25% more productive than other comparable plants who do not use teams. GE has made teams a corporate goal. Robert Erskine, manager of production resources was quoted as saying, "We're trying radically to reduce the work cycle needed to produce a product, when you combine automation with new systems and work teams, you get a 40% to 50% improvement in productivity."

In 1985 **AT & T** created a subsidiary in Morristown, NJ which provides financing for customers who lease equipment from AT & T and other companies. Traditionally, these back-office clerical employees labor at repetitive, monotonous, narrowly defined jobs. Instead of organizing in this manner where one department handles applications, another checks credit, another works on contracts, and yet another collects payments, 11 self-directed teams were set-up. Team members were made responsible for solving customers' problems and members could decide how to deal with customers, schedule work, and interview new employees. Giving people more responsibility and autonomy has made a difference. Workers now know how their job fits into the overall plan to satisfy customers. The teams have a bonus plan tied to profits and pay-for-skills. The results are that teams now process twice as many applications as they did under the old system, and in half the time it used to take. And ATCC is growing.

★

Notes:

Questions:

What are the compelling "Economic Realities" for your company (or your division of a company)?

_____

_____

_____

_____

What is driving the change towards teams?

_____

_____

_____

_____

If you already have teams, how are they designed/organized?

_____

_____

_____

_____

Chapter 2

Characteristics of Successful Self-Directed Work Teams

What are they?
How are they different from
traditional work, and how are
they designed and implemented?

Self-Directed Work Teams is a relatively new name for a form of employee involvement that has its origins in the 1950s. What we see now is a rapid increase in the companies using or planning to implement SDWTs because they are so ideally suited to today's workplace. They fit what workers and organizations want.

Today's Workers Want:

More Responsibility
More Authority
More Skills and Training
More Decision-Making Power
More Information
More Influence
More Rewards—both intrinsic (the work itself) and extrinsic (recognition, praise, money based on performance)

And Organizations Want and Need:

Workers More Responsible for Quality and Cost-Savings
Continuous Improvement — Everyone, Improving Everything, Every Day
More Flexible, Multi-Skilled Workers
More Empowered Workers Able to Serve Customers
Faster Cycle Times
Everyone Working "Smarter"
Constant Change & Innovation
Proactive Not Reactive Culture
Everyone Acting Like an "Owner" (Motivated, Committed, Empowered)

Definition:

This concept goes by many different names: Self-Directed Work Teams, Self-Managing Teams, High-Involvement Workforce, etc. The teams themselves vary depending on what makes sense to the work of the organization. **A general definition, therefore, is a group of employees (anywhere from 5-15 on the average) who are responsible for a whole product or process. The team plans the work and performs it, managing many of the things supervision or management used to do.**

The team meets regularly (once a week or every day) to identify, analyze, and solve problems. They may schedule, set goals, give performance feedback, hire, fire, etc. The team's duties grow with their skills. They aren't expected to do all these things at the beginning; their responsibilities are increased as their new skills are mastered and the team grows and develops.

SDWTs vary depending on what

makes sense to the type of work being performed, but generally, they share the following characteristics:

- Members possess a variety of technical skills. (They have been trained to be multi-skilled and able to perform each other's jobs.)
- They are accountable for production, quality, costs and schedules (in some teams members interview and hire new people, do appraisals, make repairs, monitor statistical process control, coordinate with other departments, etc.).
- Members have (with the help of training) interpersonal skills that teamwork requires (communication, feedback, problem-solving, decision-making, etc.).
- The team is constantly encouraged to increase skills, improve the product or service, and solve problems.

Questions:

What is my organization calling the teams?

_____

_____

_____

_____

_____

How is my organization defining a SDWT? (Size, job duties, skills, etc.)

_____

_____

_____

_____

_____

SDWTs Are Different From Traditional Work

1. Teams of multi-skilled employees are responsible for doing a whole job (an entire piece of work or a process) and accountable for producing specified end results.

2. Quality control and routine maintenance are part of the team's responsibilities not separate functions.

3. The teams schedule which members will do a task; some assign rotating tasks.

4. Leadership is shared; not performed by a supervisor (if there is a designated Team or Group Leader, he/she is more of a facilitator supporting the group as coach and trainer rather than the traditional "boss").

5. Customer satisfaction and business goals are the focus, therefore SDWTs need information and feedback on quantity, quality, scheduling, cost, etc. In other words, information traditionally reserved for management is supplied directly to the team so it can establish goals and monitor progress.

6. SDWTs meet regularly (some daily, some weekly) to solve problems and in this way be self-correcting. Team meetings are spent: diagnosing, analyzing, and solving complex problems, reviewing workloads, giving work assignments, and reviewing performance.

7. Members receive training in: technical skills, interpersonal skills, team skills, and administrative skills.

8. SDWT members develop trust, candor, and caring for each other.

9. People are paid for skills and productivity, not just time.

10. A "can do" attitude that grows out of commitment, involvement and having a say is at the heart of the philosophical difference.

Notes:

Questions:

How is this (or how is this going to be) different from my old job?

_____

_____

_____

_____

_____

_____

How do I feel right now about this change?

_____

_____

_____

_____

_____

_____

What do I see as the pluses and the minuses of SDWTs over traditonal work?

_____

_____

_____

_____

_____

_____

Design & Implementation of SDWTs

There is no *one* way of designing and implementing SDWTs because in order to be successful this has to be a *participative process*. You may, in visiting sites, see a design you like, but avoid the impulse to impose this on the people in your company. That's a "program" and it probably won't work for the following reasons:

1. No two companies or organizations are alike. Design a plan that fits your organization and your people.

2. Participation requires everyone's input and that means a design that is unique.

3. People tend to resist what they're not involved in designing. Asking people to participate in the planning and implementation not only taps everyone's expertise, but it gets *everyone's* buy-in. Remember a good plan is only good if people will carry it out.

4. You need everyone's ideas and expertise to develop a sound plan. No one person or even a small group can think of everything.

5. If you dictate a plan, your actions will contradict the very things you're trying to accomplish. Your actions will speak louder than your words and defeat the very thing you want to bring about.

Where do you start? The following design process has been used with success. It provides just enough structure while still being participatory.

■ Both start-ups and redesigns begin with a lot of reading, talking, and visiting other sites to see how SDWTs really work. A **Sponsor** (usually top management) starts the process by seeing a problem or an opportunity that work redesign could address.
• The process can start anywhere in the organization but unless top management supports the process with money, resources, time, etc. it cannot succeed for very long without hitting insurmountable barriers.
• If there is top management support, workers, managers, technical people, supervisors, etc. begin a dialogue and look at the entire organization.

■ **A Steering Committee** is then appointed made up of top management, union officials (if there is a union), and other key people (workers, engineers, supervisors, managers, team leaders, etc.) The steering committee discusses the philosophy and values this new system will embody and how things will be different from the traditional workplace. Team building for this group is helpful in order for people to feel open and honest about their thoughts and feelings concerning this new venture. Visiting other companies together also builds rapport. A consultant can be helpful in facilitating the process.
■ The Steering Committee selects the portion of the organization to redesign and then appoints one or more design teams to look at the entire present system and suggest ways it can be redesigned to optimize productivity. Members of the **Design Team** should be representative of all levels and functions so that each part of the organization feels part of the process.

The Design Team usually consists of:
- Some members of the Steering Committee
- Key managers/supervisors/ team leaders
- Key functional people with technical expertise
- Workers from the redesigned area

Typically the Design Team does the following:

1. Looks at the needs of outside customers, vendors, the government, etc. who exert an external influence on the organization. The team examines how the organization is presently responding to these environmental demands.

2. Looks at how the present system works technically. The team studies how the entire system functions: how and where errors occur, raw materials needed, quality requirements, etc. and what needs to be redesigned.

3. Looks at how the present system works socially and how redesign could create: increased job satisfaction, job enrichment, job coordination, cross-functional relationships, leadership and supporting roles.

4. Examines every aspect of the current system: hiring, firing, training, planning, scheduling, compensating, repairing, etc. and looks for oppor-

tunities to improve these things in agreement with the new philosophy and values the new system will embody.

5. Spends time reading, taking courses, talking and interviewing people, and visiting other companies that are already working this way.

6. Gives periodic presentations to steering and other groups on the status of their findings and receives valuable feedback on various work design proposals under consideration. Everyone's involvement here is important. People who actually do the work need to say how feasible the new design is. Free and open discussions are crucial to getting everyone's involvement and ultimately, everyone's commitment to the new design.

7. Prepares a design and implementation proposal. Three months is about the average time a design team takes to get to this point. This plan is discussed with all affected parties before it is approved by the Steering Committee.

8. Usually a pilot group is then chosen either by asking for a group of volunteers who want to do this or by picking a group because they meet certain criteria and would have the best chance of succeeding. Then, other teams are added gradually.

9. The Design Team phase usually takes an average of 3-6 months depending on whether the members work at redesigning full- or part-time.

Important Redesign Considerations:

- Each organization has to create an original design that uniquely fits their workplace. It has to make sense to everyone and take into account what is best for the process and the people.

- This socio-tech process of designing better work for everyone has worked in new sites and redesigns of traditional factories and offices (with union and non-union workforces).

- Fragmented jobs are turned into whole tasks that a team completes for its customers.

- The aim is for everyone to understand how the whole system works and to be empowered to act on behalf of a customer.

- Action-orientation is the goal. High-quality decisions can be made swiftly by teams of highly committed workers who are empowered to do what is right.

- Everybody's job will change.

- Designs should include a responsibility chart which shows how the team will, over time, take over the tasks performed by staff and supervision. This transition plan helps everyone receive training and gradually adjust to new roles in the organization.

- This process of establishing this new way of working usually takes a minimum of 2-3 years in order for gains in productivity, quality, and job satisfaction to take effect.

- This is a very exciting and frustrating time. Not everyone can work in this new environment and options should be available to everyone.

Questions:

1. Is your organization a start-up or redesign?

_____

_____

_____

_____

_____

_____

2. Do you have a steering committee?

_____

_____

...design team?

_____

_____

...a pilot group?

_____

_____

...several SDWTs?

_____

_____

3. How would you assess progress thus far? (moving too fast, too slowly, just right, etc.)

_____

_____

_____

_____

_____

_____

4. If you have a pilot team, what has been the reaction to it?

_____

_____

_____

_____

_____

5. Is there a transition plan in place?

_____

_____

_____

_____

_____

6. What has been a success thus far?

_____

_____

_____

_____

_____

7. What has been a problem?

_____

_____

_____

_____

_____

8. What is the general reaction to all this change on the part of the average worker?

_____

_____

_____

_____

_____

...The average supervisor?

_____

_____

_____

_____

_____

_____

...The average manager?

_____

_____

_____

_____

_____

...Support person?

_____

_____

_____

_____

_____

Chapter **3**

How "Teams" Are Different From Groups

**Key elements of
effective teamwork
and a "Team Assessment"**

INDIVIDUAL
EXERCISE

*What has been the best team experience you've ever had (either at work or outside
of work)? (Describe it.)*

_____

_____

_____

_____

What made it the best team experience? (List the characteristics.)

_____   _____

_____   _____

_____   _____

_____   _____

When everyone has finished, discuss this with the team.

For several years we've been asking people in our workshops to answer
the same questions you just answered and what they've been telling us
agrees with the research on what makes teams different from groups. Let's
see how your list compares with characteristics on the next page.

Successful Teams Have:

1. A SHARED GOAL/MISSION THAT EVERYONE KNOWS AND AGREES ON AND IS COMMITTED TO ACCOMPLISHING. The team members understand the goals because they have participated in setting them. There is a lot of discussion of the task and how to best accomplish it. Everyone feels a high degree of involvement. Each member feels that he/she makes a difference to the overall result.

2. A CLIMATE OF TRUST AND OPENNESS. The team creates a climate where members are comfortable and informal. Trust replaces fear and people are able and willing to take risks. It is a growth and learning climate where people are involved and interested.

3. OPEN AND HONEST COMMUNICATION. Team members feel free to express their thoughts, feelings, and ideas. Members listen to each other and everyone feels free to put forth an idea without being criticized or embarrassed. Conflict and disagreement are viewed as natural and dealt with. The team self-corrects by giving feedback to members on how they affect the team (positively or negatively) in meeting or not meeting its goals.

4. A SENSE OF BELONGING to the team and commitment to its actions. There is a sense of participation and a high-level of involvement. Out of this sense of inclusion ("I am an important part of this team and what I do makes a difference") comes high-commitment and pride in the team's accomplishments.

5. DIVERSITY VALUED AS AN ASSET. Team members are viewed as unique people with valuable resources. Diversity of opinions, ideas, and experience is encouraged rather than practicing "Groupthink" where differences are viewed as deviance from the norm. Flexibility and sensitivity to others is practiced.

6. CREATIVITY AND RISK-TAKING ARE ENCOURAGED. Team members are encouraged to take risks, try something different instead of "SOW" (doing it the "same old way"). Mistakes are seen as part of learning through experimentation. Constant improvement can only take place if people are encouraged to try new ways and make suggestions on improvements without being punished.

7. ABILITY TO SELF-CORRECT. The team is able to constantly improve itself by examining its processes and practices. The team looks periodically at what may be interfering with its operations. Open discussion attempts to find the causes of problems whether they are procedures, individual behavior, etc. and the team develops solutions instead of letting problems worsen.

8. MEMBERS WHO ARE INTERDEPENDENT. They need each other's knowledge, skill, and resources to produce something together they could not do as well alone.

9. CONSENSUS DECISION-MAKING. Members of the team make decisions together that are of high-quality and have the acceptance and support of the entire team to carry them out.

10. **PARTICIPATIVE LEADERSHIP.** Whether the group has a designated leader or leadership shifts among the members, the leader does not dominate the group. Everyone is used as a resource.

The role of the leader is one of facilitator:

- Listening to Team Members
- Creating a Climate of Trust and Openness
- Eliminating Fear
- Valuing Diversity
- Role-Modeling ("Walking-the-Talk;" Practicing what he or she Preaches)
- Communicating the Goal and Mission of the Organization
- Delegating, Coaching, Counseling, and Teaching
- Encouraging Creativity, Risk-taking, and Constant Improvement of Everything by Everyone
- Sharing Information
- Motivating
- Empowering People (making people more able to do their job and serve the customer - better, faster, and with quality).
- Helping the Team become more and more self-directed (Less dependent on the Leader)
- Using Feedback to help the group self-correct by examining its procedures
- Dealing with Conflict
- Keeping the Team on Track
- Leading Effective Meetings
- Handling Personality Conflicts
- Developing the Team (by Understanding Group Dynamics)
- Managing Their Boss
- Influencing without Authority
- Breaking Down Cross-Functional Barriers

Notes:

Team-Building Assessment:

Circle the number that best describes where you believe the Team is "NOW" in regard to each of these items.

Scale: 0 = Never, 1 = Some of the Time, 2 = Most of the time, 3 = Always

(If an item does not apply, do not answer it.)

	Never	Some of the Time	Most of the Time	Always
1. Trust Between Team Members.	0	1	2	3
2. Members trust Team Leader.	0	1	2	3
3. Team Leader Trusts Team Members.	0	1	2	3
4. Support for Team from Upper Level Management.	0	1	2	3
5. Team Members Listen to Each Other.	0	1	2	3
6. Team Leader is a Good Listener.	0	1	2	3
7. Team Members Openly & Honestly Communicate Their Thoughts and Feelings.	0	1	2	3
8. Team Listens To My Ideas.	0	1	2	3
9. Team Uses My Ideas.	0	1	2	3
10. Team Receives the Information It Needs to be Effective.	0	1	2	3
11. Team Receives the Technical Training It Needs.	0	1	2	3
12. Team Receives the Interpersonal Training It Needs.	0	1	2	3
13. Team Meetings are Effective.	0	1	2	3
—Time is Well Spent.	0	1	2	3
—Problems Are Discussed.	0	1	2	3
—Problems Are Solved.	0	1	2	3
Total				

	Never	Some of the Time	Most of the Time	Always
—Actions are Taken Following The Meeting.	0	1	2	3
—New Ideas Are Encouraged.	0	1	2	3
—Everyone Attends.	0	1	2	3
—No One Dominates.	0	1	2	3
—Consensus is Reached.	0	1	2	3
—Feedback is Used So The Team Can Self-Correct.	0	1	2	3
14. Everyone On The Team Knows The Mission and Goals.	0	1	2	3
15. Everyone On The Team Agrees With and Supports The Mission and Goals.	0	1	2	3
16. Everyone Has Input On Setting The Mission and Goals.	0	1	2	3
17. The Team Is Productive.	0	1	2	3
18. The Team Is Very Participative (Everyone Is Involved In Making Consensus Decisions).	0	1	2	3
19. Everyone Supports Decisions Once They Are Made.	0	1	2	3
20. Everyone Supports The Team Leader's Decisions.	0	1	2	3
21. Conflict is Constructive.	0	1	2	3
22. There is No "Group Think" (People Agreeing Just To Go Along With Majority and Not Make Waves).	0	1	2	3
23. The Team Feels Responsible For Carrying Out Decisions.	0	1	2	3
24. There Is Little or No Win-Lose Competition Between Members.	0	1	2	3
Total				

	Never	Some of the Time	Most of the Time	Always
25. Team Members Understand Each Other's Goals and Problems.	0	1	2	3
26. Team Members Get The Help They Need From Each Other.	0	1	2	3
27. Team Members Get The Help They Need From Support People.	0	1	2	3
28. Team Members Stick-Up For Each Other.	0	1	2	3
29. The Team Leader Sticks-Up For Team Members.	0	1	2	3
30. Team Members Stick-Up For The Team Leader.	0	1	2	3
31. I Feel Free To Take Risks.	0	1	2	3
32. I Feel Secure In My Job.	0	1	2	3
33. I Feel Close To The Team Members.	0	1	2	3
34. I Feel Close To The Team Leader.	0	1	2	3
35. I Feel Productive.	0	1	2	3
36. I Feel Rewarded For My Work.	0	1	2	3
37. I Feel Recognized For My Efforts.	0	1	2	3
38. The Team Receives The Recognition It Deserves From Management.	0	1	2	3
39. The Team Leader:				
—Teaches	0	1	2	3
—Coaches	0	1	2	3
—Counsels	0	1	2	3
Total				

	Never	Some of the Time	Most of the Time	Always
40. Team Members:				
—Teach Each Other	0	1	2	3
—Coach Each Other	0	1	2	3
—Counsel Each Other	0	1	2	3
41. The Team Gets The Time It Needs To Develop Itself and Solve Problems.	0	1	2	3
42. I Feel I'm Learning and Growing On This Job.	0	1	2	3
43. There Are Adequate Career Paths For Me.	0	1	2	3
44. I Feel I Can Influence (Make A Difference To):				
—The Team	0	1	2	3
—Management	0	1	2	3
—Other Functions	0	1	2	3
—The Entire Organization/Company	0	1	2	3
45. We Have An Effective Suggestion System.	0	1	2	3
46. We Are Constantly Improving Things.	0	1	2	3
47. We Are Constantly Learning.	0	1	2	3
48. We Think "Customer" All The Time.	0	1	2	3
49. We Receive Regular, Systematic Feedback From Our Customers.	0	1	2	3
50. There Is A Lot of Cross-Functional Cooperation.	0	1	2	3
51. Problems Between Team Members Are Confronted and Addressed By The Team.	0	1	2	3
52. The Team Has Fun Together.	0	1	2	3
Total				

	Never	Some of the Time	Most of the Time	Always
53. I Feel Motivated.	0	1	2	3
54. I Feel Committed.	0	1	2	3
55. I Feel Loyal To This Company.	0	1	2	3

The Blank Lines are for adding your own questions.

	Never	Some of the Time	Most of the Time	Always
56. _____	0	1	2	3
57. _____	0	1	2	3
58. _____	0	1	2	3

	Never	Some of the Time	Most of the Time	Always
Total				
Total of All Columns				
Grand Total				

Notes:

TEAM EXERCISE

After each team member has completed the ''Team-Building Assessment,'' ask everyone to:

1. Indicate their scores by a show of hands. (Example: ''Raise your hand if you rated Question #1: Trust Between Team Members as a ''0''. Raise your hand if you rated Question #1 with a ''1'' …a ''2'', …a ''3''?)

■ The entire team can then discuss each question after each show of hands or you can go through the entire list and then have an open discussion of the ones that received high and low scores from the team.

2. Discuss your grand totals. Is there a large difference in their range?

3. As a team brainstorm actions you feel should be taken to build the team. (''Guidelines for Brainstorming'' on next page.)

_____	_____
_____	_____
_____	_____
_____	_____
_____	_____
_____	_____
_____	_____
_____	_____
_____	_____
_____	_____

4. After you've generated a list, prioritize it by deciding as a team which one or two things you want to do now, which later, etc.

Guidelines for Brainstorming:

1. Call out anything that pops into your mind.

2. Put everything said on a flip chart (if something is repeated add it also).

3. No discussion.

4. No judgement.

5. Silence is O.K. (just wait patiently without saying anything and more ideas might come forth).

6. Adding ideas onto other people's ideas is fine and should be encouraged.

7. Be creative (anything goes).

8. Have fun!

Notes:

Chapter 4

Setting Team Ground Rules & Examining Norms

One of the first things a group has to do to develop into a TEAM is to reach agreement on operating ground rules. If your team already has established ground rules, then it's time to examine team norms

INDIVIDUAL EXERCISE

Assumptions About Teams

Instructions: PART I - INDIVIDUAL TASK - Read each statement once. Check whether you agree (A) or disagree (D) with each statement.

Key: "A" if you agree; "D" if you disagree.

(   ) 1. A primary concern of all team members should be to establish an atmosphere where all are free to express their opinions.

(   ) 2. In a team with a strong leader, an individual is able to achieve greater personal security than in a team with a more passive leader.

(   ) 3. There are often occasions when an individual who is part of a working team should do what he/she thinks is right regardless of what the group has decided to do.

(   ) 4. Members should be required to attend team meetings.

(   ) 5. Generally, there comes a time when democratic group methods must be abandoned in order to solve practical problems.

(   ) 6. In the long run, it is more important to use involvement/participative methods than to achieve specific results by other means.

(   ) 7. Sometimes it is necessary to change people in the direction you yourself think is right, even when they object.

(   ) 8. It is sometimes necessary to ignore the feelings of others in order to reach a group decision.

Continued on next page

(   ) 9. When leaders are doing their best, one should not openly criticize or find fault with their conduct.

(   ) 10. Meetings would be more productive if the leader would get quickly to the point and say what he/she wants the group to do.

(   ) 11. By the time the average person has reached maturity, it is almost impossible for him/her to increase his/her skill in group participation.

(   ) 12. Interest falls off when everybody in the group has to be considered before making decisions.

(   ) 13. Teamwork increases when the leader is careful to choose friends as team members.

(   ) 14. A team is no stronger than its weakest member.

(   ) 15. In the long run, it is more productive to replace an ineffective team member than to try and retrain him/her.

(   ) 16. Once a team gets established in a set way of working, it is almost impossible to change.

(   ) 17. When a team gets a new leader, the whole pattern of the team changes.

(   ) 18. One resistant team member can keep a whole team from improving its performance.

(   ) 19. The most important condition in a successful team building program is the motivation level of the team members to want to see the program succeed.

(   ) 20. To become a really effective team, members should have a personal liking for each other.

(   ) 21. A team decision is always better than an individual decision.

TEAM EXERCISE

PART 2: When everyone has finished, discuss your individual answers and then reach consensus* on whether you agree or disagree with each statement. (You can change the wording of the statements in order to reach consensus.)

*Guidelines for Reaching Consensus:

1. Make sure everyone is heard from and feels listened to.

2. Do not vote — your aim is to talk through the issue until you've reached an agreement everyone can support.

3. Consensus may not mean that you are in 100% agreement, but you've been heard and you'll support the team's decision.

4. Do not give in just to reach agreement—view conflict and differences of opinion as good.

5. Be open. Strive for a creative solution.

6. Ask questions and make sure you understand everyone's opinion before you make up your mind.

Team Ground Rules

The statements you just discussed are good vehicles for getting to know each other and the opinions you have that make you unique. Everyone's opinion needs to be heard. You probably learned that in many cases even your definitions of words were different. You probably had to change some wording in order to finally agree, and in the process you might have come out with a statement that is even better than the original one.

Every team needs to engage in the process of establishing its own ground rules (mutually agreed on ways of conducting itself). Teams will vary in this because the people are different and in a lot of ways the rules don't matter as long as the team members agree on them.

The process of reaching consensus on these matters is very important (in other words, how you do it is as critical as the results). Each person needs to be listened to. If some members are quiet, they need to be drawn out. If other people are exerting too much influence, they need to listen more and talk less.

The final results of consensus will not be that everyone agrees 100%, but rather they have been heard and can live with the ground rules and will support them. If anyone cannot, or will not, support the final results—the team isn't finished and must talk more. Ground rules are meaningless unless all team members buy into and live them.

THE PURPOSE OF TEAM GROUND RULES

- To express the values of the Team.

- To make sure every Team Member knows and agrees with what's expected of him or her.

- To develop norms that support the needs of the Team Members and the needs of the organization.

- To help the Team evaluate its performance.

- To help a new Team Member know what's expected of him or her.

- To have everyone agree on what's important to the Team and provide a guide for behavior.

A new team needs to discuss and decide on ground rules for issues like these:

1. How often shall we hold team meetings?
   - How long should they be? When? Where?
   - How should we establish the agenda?
   - Who is going to chair the meetings? Take minutes?
2. How are we going to get feedback and measure our performance?
3. What is our goal/purpose as a team?
4. How can we best accomplish our mission? What ground rules do we all agree would help us accomplish our goals?
5. What are our expectations for the team? (Each of our biggest worries? Hopes? Past experiences with teams?)
6. How will we make decisions?
7. Resolve problems? Handle conflicts?
8. How do we make sure everyone is listened to and everyone has a say?
9. How will we handle time constraints?
10. How will we prioritize our work?
11. How will we measure our productivity? Quality?
12. How will we self-correct (look at what we're doing that is productive and not and make corrections)?
13. What kind of climate do we want in our group? How can we build the kind of climate we want?
14. How can we constantly improve what we do?
15. What skills do members have and which do they want to learn? How are we going to build cross-training into our schedule?
16. What other kinds of operating guidelines do we need to formulate? (attendance, tardiness, vacation, scheduling, etc.)

_____

_____

_____

TEAM EXERCISE

Setting Ground Rules

Step I. What are some ground rules our team needs to agree on? Have each person write one ground rule he/she feels is important.

_____

Step II. Ask each person to read their answers and write them here:

1. _____
2. _____
3. _____
4. _____
5. _____
6. _____
7. _____
8. _____
9. _____
10. _____
11. _____
12. _____
13. _____

Step III. Next, as a team discuss the entire list eliminating or changing any item. Reach consensus* on the ones the team wants to adopt as its ground rules. (List your final "Team Ground Rules" on the back of this page.)

*"Guidelines for Reaching Consensus" on page 37.

Our Team's Ground Rules:

TEAM EXERCISE

Examining Team Norms

What is agreed on is a ground rule; what actually happens is a norm. Unlike ground rules, norms are *unwritten* rules of behavior which impact how we work together. All groups have norms, but usually these norms are not discussed and so are unconscious.

Step I. As a Team brainstorm* the Norms you have as a Team:
Write them in the column on the left.

Norm:	Impact:
Example: Our meetings start on time.	*Some members miss the first few minutes.*

*"Guidelines for Brainstorming" on page 32.

Step II. After the Team has completed the list of norms, discuss it as a Team and reach agreement on which ones are truly your norms.

Step III. Lastly, agree on and list in the column to the right the "Impact" of each norm.

Questions:

After you've reached agreement on your final list of norms, answer the following questions:

1. How do these norms agree or disagree with our stated ground rules?

_____

_____

_____

_____

2. Which norms do we want to change or modify? Why?

Norm _____

Reason for Changing _____

Norm _____

Reason for Changing _____

Norm _____

Reason for Changing _____

3. Any other thoughts concerning Team Norms or Ground Rules?

_____

_____

_____

_____

Chapter 5

Characteristics of the Effective Team Member

**The qualities and skills one needs
to develop in order to be an
effective Team Member: A Self-Assessment**

Self-Assessment: How Do You Rate As A Team Member?

(Rate yourself on a scale of 0-3 on how often you exhibit the following characteristics.)
Circle the best answer.

1. I understand, support and feel ownership for the Team's goals.

0	1	2	3
Never	Sometimes	Most of the Time	Always

2. I am willing to put the Team's goals ahead of my own. (The Team Member understands that the Team's goals and his/her personal goals are ultimately the same. He/she feels a win-win with the Team.)

0	1	2	3
Never	Sometimes	Most of the Time	Always

3. I listen to everyone on the Team. (Chapter 11 will go into the details of the kind of "Active" listening we're talking about, but briefly, we mean really understanding the other person's point of view. Being "other-person" focused and not making judgments, but attempting to understand before forming an opinion.)

0	1	2	3
Never	Sometimes	Most of the Time	Always

4. I am both "task" and "team" focused. (The Team Member knows what the goals are and wants to accomplish them, but at the same time is aware of the importance of maintaining and developing the team. Listening to everyone, using conflict constructively, reaching consensus, working for harmony when possible, maintaining good relationships with everyone, compromising when necessary, etc. are all behaviors that make sure the goal/task is accomplished in a manner that does not damage the Team.)

0	1	2	3
Never	Sometimes	Most of the Time	Always

5. I see conflict as useful and necessary. (The Team Member doesn't create conflict for the excitement of it, but also doesn't suppress divergent views. An effective Team avoids "group think"—a group phenomenon where people agree to do something no one thinks is a good idea because no one wants to create conflict. This can be avoided by voicing honest opinions and presenting pertinent facts, not just agreeing for the sake of harmony.)

0	1	2	3
Never	Sometimes	Most of the Time	Always

6. I trust the other members of the Team. (The Team Member works at getting to know and understand everyone. He/she shares their honest thoughts and feelings to build trust. If he/she senses a lack a trust in a Team relationship, a conscious choice is made to do something that begins to change the relationship and not just maintain the status quo.)

0	1	2	3
Never	Sometimes	Most of the Time	Always

7. I communicate openly and honestly.

0	1	2	3
Never	Sometimes	Most of the Time	Always

8. I respect differences and value diversity. (People are unique; no two are alike. While we know this intellectually, we also, at times, make the mistaken assumption that we are all the same. Team Members need to spend time understanding each other's similarities, but most especially differences because all of us want others to know and accept our uniqueness. Stereotyping, judging and false assumptions all get in the way of seeing people as they really are and appreciating their diversity. It would be a dull world if we were all alike. A Team needs people with different viewpoints who will think of different ideas, suggestions, innovations, etc.)

0	1	2	3
Never	Sometimes	Most of the Time	Always

9. I work for consensus. (Critical to teamwork is the idea that members have a say, everyone listens and out of that process a general agreement is reached. It doesn't mean that each member is in unanimous agreement with the decision, but rather that he/she feels they've been heard, involved, and they will now support and carry-out the Team's decision.)

0	1	2	3
Never	Sometimes	Most of the Time	Always

10. I utilize the resources of others. (An effective Team Member knows what strengths, knowledge, skills other members have and works at tapping those skills for the best of the Team. He/she also knows what skills each member is trying to develop and helps them achieve those goals. Periodically, self-directed work teams need to self-correct, that is, look at how the team is helping or hindering members' growth and development and adjust its procedures if it is having a negative impact on people. A Team is only as effective as its members.)

0	1	2	3
Never	Sometimes	Most of the Time	Always

Total [   ] **(A Perfect Score is 30.)**

Action Commitments:

1. Based on your answers to this Self-Assessment, what "Action Commitments" do you want to make at this time to further develop your skills as a Team Member?

_____

_____

_____

_____

_____

_____

2. Is there some training you feel would be helpful to you?

_____

_____

_____

_____

_____

_____

_____

_____

TEAM EXERCISE

Pairings

Have every member of the team pair with one other person. In these pairs discuss your answers to the "Self-Assessment/Action Commitments." (Make sure each of you shares "air time" and "actively" listens.)

Chapter 6

Measuring Your Team

Assessments for determining
how self-directed your
team really is
on 3 dimensions

Dimension #1: What Operational Tasks/Responsibilities Are Handled by Your Team?

Who Does This Now?			Check One (✔)	
Tasks/Responsibilities:	Team's Responsibility	Shared Responsibility (Team Leader* & Team)	Team Leader's* Responsibility	Management's Responsibility
Maintaining Safety & Housekeeping				
Setting Operational Goals for Team				
Measuring Quality				
Measuring Customer Service				
Working with Internal Customers				
Working with External Customers				
Working with Vendors/Suppliers				
Selecting Work Methods				
Implementing Process Improvements				
Performing Routine Maintenance				
Stopping Work Process to Address Quality Concerns				
Assigning Daily Tasks to Team Members				
Preparing & Managing Budgets				
Production Control & Work Scheduling				
Other_____				
_____				
_____				

*Team Leader's Role may have a different name: Supervisor, Group Leader, Resource, Facilitator, etc.

Dimension #2: What Administrative Tasks/Responsibilities Are Handled by Your Team?

Who Does This Now?				*Check one (✔)*
Tasks/Responsibilities:	Team's Responsibility	Shared Responsibility (Team Leader & Team)	Team Leader's* Responsibility	Management's Responsibility
Vacation Scheduling				
Performance Appraisals				
Individual Performance Problems				
Selection of Team Members				
Hiring New Employees				
Firing Employees				
Determining Training Needs				
Addressing Training Needs				
Cross-Training Each Other				
Compensation Decisions				
Other_____				
_____				
_____				

Dimension #3: What Types of Training Has Your Team Received To Date?

Instructions: Place a check (√) next to items your team has already received training in. Place date in column for training planned.	Training Received (√)	Training Planned (Date)
New Roles & Responsibilities in SDWTs		
Problem-Solving Skills		
Quality Concepts		
Using Quality Tools		
Work Flow Analysis		
Presentation Skills		
Group Dynamics Skills		
Budgeting		
Selecting Team Members		
Decision-making Skills		
Communication Skills		
Conflict Management		
Measuring & Evaluating Team Performance		
Effective Meeting Skills		
Technical Skills Training (includes Cross-Training)		
Other_____		
_____		
_____		
_____		
_____		

TEAM EXERCISE

Summary/Discussion

After your team has discussed all 3 dimensions, answer the following questions.

1. Regarding Dimensions 1 & 2, is there a transition plan in place to keep adding tasks/responsibilities to the team? (For example, if budgeting is now being done by the Team Leader, is there a plan to eventually teach the team about budgeting so they can one day take over that responsibility?) If there is no transition plan, should there be?

_____

_____

_____

_____

_____

_____

2. Discuss Dimension #3 together. Has the team received the kind of training it needs? Is there a transition plan in place to supply the kind of training that is and will be needed?

_____

_____

_____

_____

_____

_____

Measuring & Evaluating How the Team Is Doing

Teams need feedback in order to know how they're doing so they can "self-correct" and improve their processes. How to measure and evaluate, therefore, is very important.

There is no one best way to do this. Each organization is unique and needs to involve its people in defining a measurement and evaluation system that works for them. Typically, companies have not been very effective in this area.

> In 1991 a survey conducted by the American Productivity & Quality Center found that almost 40 percent of the 417 people surveyed said their performance was not evaluated in a fair manner.

Self-directed teams attempt to address this problem by involving people in designing systems that provide accurate feedback. **The best measurement systems include the following features:**

■ Focusing on what's important to a customer (both internal and external). If you don't know, find out and use a variety of methods (face-to-face, questionnaires, 800 numbers, etc.)

■ Measuring the Team's performance by gathering feedback on things like:

  • Production (yield, number of customer complaints, etc.)

  • Maintaining the Technical System (machines, maintenance, etc.)

  • Customer Service

  • Safety

  • Relations with Supplier/Vendors

  • Quality

  • Team Development

■ Team Measurements based on Team goals that fit into the department/division/company goals

■ The Team sets individual performance standards for team members. Examples are:
  • Knowledge of multiple jobs
  • Performs a task accurately (error-free)
  • Completes work on time
  • Problem-solving
  • Continuously improves
  • Learns and develops
  • Is a good team member (cooperates with others, helps others, participates, has good relationships with others, shows commitment to self-directed work team concept, etc.)
  • Attends meetings and gets involved
  • Uses time well
  • Demonstrates creativity
  • Is a Leader at times
  • Has good interpersonal skills (communication, listening, etc.)
  • Technical skills proficiency
  • Attendance

■ Reward and compensation systems are tied to measurement and evaluation. (More on reward systems in Chapter 14.)

Peer Assessments

Self-directed teams do not usually have peer assessments until the team has been together for a period of time. When peers do assess each other certain assumptions are made about the benefits of peer assessment over traditional forms of appraisal:

- Peers know each other better.

- Peers can really see how each other works (both technically and as a team member).

- Peers will provide several raters, not just one opinion, therefore, a fairer assessment.

- Peers have most to gain or lose by providing fair, accurate feedback.

- Peer pressure will be a powerful motivator.

- Peers know and see each other's strengths and areas to develop.

We are seeing more peer assessment as more and more companies move to team-based cultures. Some companies have been doing this for quite awhile and we need to learn from their experiences.

Companies Using Peer Review*

GORE & ASSOCIATES has been using peer reviews since the company was started in 1958. Every employee is ranked on the basis of his/her contribution to the company goals and paid accordingly. The ranking is done by a compensation committee at each Gore facility (about 40 plants each with no more than 200 people) made up of 6-10 workers, with input from peers and customers. These "contribution lists" as they're called, are compiled several times a year.

QUAKER OATS PET FOOD'S entire performance appraisal process is made up of peer review. SDWTs make all compensation and promotion decisions on this basis. Peers evaluate how well each person is doing in terms of the work processes and, equally important, how effective they are as a team member (spirit, communication, problem-solving, etc.) They use a pay-for-knowledge compensation system that rewards people for learning new skills.

*As reported in "An Early Review of Peer Review," *Training Magazine*, July 1991.

Questions:

1. How does your team currently get feedback?

_____

_____

_____

_____

_____

_____

_____

2. What does your team currently measure?

_____

_____

_____

_____

_____

_____

3. Are there other dimensions the team should be measuring? (Teamwork, customer service, etc.)

_____

_____

_____

_____

_____

_____

Chapter 7

The Role of
The Team Leader

**Whether your Team has a designated
Team Leader or leadership shifts
among all the members,
you'll find that SDWTs require
a different type of leadership role**

INDIVIDUAL EXERCISE

Think for a minute about the most effective leader you've ever worked with. What qualities did he/she possess? Write them here:

_____   _____

_____   _____

_____   _____

_____   _____

_____   _____

_____   _____

_____   _____

TEAM EXERCISE

When every Team Member has finished their list of qualities, discuss this as a Team. Reach consensus* on a list of qualities.

_____

_____

_____

_____

_____

_____

*"Guidelines for Consensus" are on page 37.

We've been posing this question for years to the people in our workshops. This has been a very diverse group of men and women, various ethnic groups, from all parts of the country, and at all levels of organizations—yet the answers are always strikingly similar. The following characteristics are on the vast majority of lists:

Qualities of Effective Leaders

- **Honest & Trusted**
- **Good Listener, Communicator**
- **Cared about the Work and the People**
- **Believed in me—had Positive Expectations**
- **Competent and Respected**
- **Led By Example—Words and Behavior Consistent**

We contend that these characteristics have always been needed by effective leaders. What is new now are the skills needed for leading a team because we haven't always worked in teams.

New Leadership Skills Needed For SDWTs:

- **Team Building**
- **Facilitating Effective Team Meetings**
- **Understanding What "True" Participation & Employee Involvement Are**
- **Facilitating Team Problem-Solving**
- **Tapping "Synergy"**

- **Understanding Group Dynamics-The Stages of Group Development and What To Do At Each Stage**
- **Managing Change**
- **Managing Diversity**
- **Communicating Mission & Goals**
- **Influencing Without Authority**
- **Building SDWTs and Other Forms of High-Involvement/High Commitment**

SDWT Leadership Assessment

In order for a team to self-direct, the role of leadership needs to be redesigned. Organizations generally do this in one of two ways. Some companies design teams where leadership shifts from member-to-member with no one person being "the leader" all the time. Other organizations designate a Team Leader (or Group Leader or Facilitator or Resource, etc.) who is responsible for the leadership of the team. Exactly what the Team Leader is responsible for varies.

Let's examine what your Team Leader is responsible for. And if you don't have a designated Team Leader, who is responsible for this activity?

INSTRUCTIONS: *Place a check (√) in column titled "Team Leader" next to the things your Team Leader is doing now. If your team does not have one designated leader, write in column titled "Other" who or what is doing this now. (Ex. Team, Mgmt., etc.)*

Leadership Activities:	Team Leader	Other
Providing Overall Direction for the Team		
Providing the Team with Resources (Space, Tools, Assistance, etc.)		
Providing Needed Business Information		
Coaching Team Members		
Facilitating Team Building Activities		
Recognizing Team Contributions		
Coordinating Between Teams/Shifts (Boundary Management; Linking)		
Coordinating With Support Groups		
Training		
Providing Technical Expertise		
Problem-solving Between Teams		
Conflict Management		
Providing Resources		
Evaluating Team Member's Performance		
Providing Inspiration (Leading by Example)		

Continued on next page

Leadership Activities:	Team Leader	Other
Championing Innovative Ideas		
Facilitating Team Meetings		
Budgeting		
Disciplining		
Hiring		
Firing		
Teaching Team to Measure & Evaluate Its Own Performance		
Fostering Continuous Improvement		
Teaching Quality Concepts		

Questions: After everyone has completed the checklist, discuss the following questions with the entire team:

1. *Are there important activities no one is doing?*

_____

_____

_____

2. *Are the right people doing the right things?*

_____

_____

_____

3. *Is there a transition plan to train team members to take on more and more leadership tasks?*

_____

_____

_____

How the Leadership Role is Different in a Self-Directed Work Team Environment vs. The Traditional Organization Model

For two-hundred years, most companies have been organized in the traditional, bureaucratic, pyramid structure.

The Shareholders, Board of Directors, and CEO were on top. Workers and customers were on the bottom. Between the two were many layers of management. This system is finally changing because its flaws are proving to be costly and even fatal. Some major flaws are:

1. This system is **slow.** It takes too long for communication, information, decision-making to go up, down and sideways. A lot of good information never gets where it should or is distorted along the way.

2. It's a **wasteful** system. It separates "thinkers" from "doers" and **quality suffers.** Too many people are checking others after mistakes have been made. This waste makes for higher costs and is no way to be competitive.

3. It is **not customer-driven** and often ignores the whole purpose of business: to serve customers. Customers who feel ignored take their business elsewhere.

4. It **doesn't respond to changing customer needs and market demands.**

5. It **fails to motivate employees** at the bottom who often have dull, fragmented jobs.

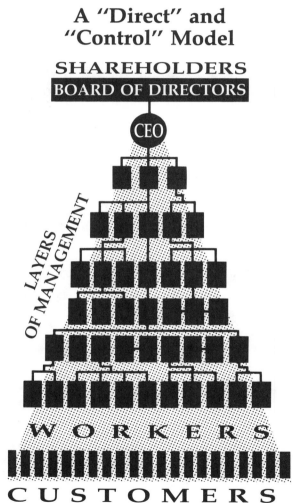

A "Direct" and "Control" Model

SHAREHOLDERS
BOARD OF DIRECTORS
CEO
LAYERS OF MANAGEMENT
W O R K E R S
C U S T O M E R S

SDWT Structure:
A High-Commitment/Performance Model

The self-directed work team structure is fast, flexible, designed to be customer-driven, and innovative. It is constantly changing and takes many forms, but generally it looks something like this:

CUSTOMERS ON TOP What the customer wants and says drives the company. Everyone listens to the customer's definition of quality and is constantly striving to meet that definition.

SELF-DIRECTED WORK TEAMS EMPOWERED to do what needs to be done in order to meet constantly changing customer demands. Multi-skilled, flexible, informed, and constantly educated/trained.

LEADERS who know how to support teams by coaching, counseling, training, removing barriers, listening, etc.

CEO who knows how to empower teams by passing on the business information, constantly providing time and money for training, giving decisions over to the people who know the most and will carry out the decisions, and making sure people are rewarded for their performance. Letting the teams take care of the day-to-day work frees the CEO and top management to make long-term, long-range plans.

CUSTOMERS ON TOP

LEADERS

CEO

BOARD OF DIRECTORS

SHAREHOLDERS

A New View Of Leadership

Leadership in the traditional hierarchy *told* people what to do and *how* to do it. Money was seen as the prime motivator. Workers were not encouraged to change things. There was no effective suggestion system. Decisions were made at the top and workers were expected to carry them out. *Thinking* and *doing* were separated.

Today's effective organization has turned the pyramid upside down. Now, customers are on top. Everyone is listening to the customer and acting on what they hear. Teams of workers are now empowered to do what needs to be done to satisfy the customer. Teams are constantly looking at what problems need to be solved: How costs can be lowered; waste and bureaucracy eliminated; things done faster, better, and smarter. Change is a constant.

Turning the pyramid upside-down requires a different state-of-mind on the part of the leader.

Effective leaders of high-performing teams must have the following kinds of beliefs, attitudes and skills:

- People are the most valuable resource any company has.
- Human beings have unlimited potential to constantly grow, develop, and learn. Helping each team member achieve his/her potential is the main role of the leader.
- Leading a high-performing team is an art and a skill.
- Teams need constant developing.
- The leader's main job is listening to people not telling them what to do and how to do it. Workers are the "experts" on the work they do.
- The leader is there to be a resource in support of the team and this means removing barriers, providing tools (whatever they might be), accessing information directly to the team/s, asking, "What do you need?" and "What can I do?"
- Everyone is capable of making decisions that affect them provided they are given the right information and training.
- The leader's role is one of teacher, coach, counselor, and trainer.
- People do not resist changes they have been involved in making.
- Real employee involvement is a "process" not a "program."
- The leader's behavior must be consistent with self-direction beliefs (the leader is a role-model of the "new" way).
- The leader must be able to "let go" in order to empower people but not "dump" on people; train and coach them first so they'll be ready and able to succeed.
- In moving towards self-direction, everyone's job changes and unless the leader changes, no one will change.
- Realize mistakes are unavoidable. Help people learn from them.
- Don't shoot the messenger. All feedback is valuable.
- Recognize, reward, and celebrate the new behaviors.

Importance of Team Leadership Supported by Research

According to a recent study of Self-Directed Work Teams,* there was a correlation between effective team leadership and positive results in terms of quality, productivity, and team member satisfaction. The following activities on the part of the supervisor or group leader were cited:

- Providing overall direction, resources, and business information to the teams

- Coaching teams to work together

- Recognizing the contributions made by the team

*Self-Directed Teams: A Study of Current Practice, a joint study by AQP, DDI, & Industry Week Magazine.

"Shared" Team Leadership

Some organizations choose not to appoint one person as the Team Leader, but instead have the leadership duties rotate among all the members. Everyone has leadership duties in addition to their regular work. Leadership for the symbol points shifts among Team Members. For example, someone receives training in safety and for the next 3 months he/she attends all the plant-wide safety meetings as the team's representative. Then, someone else is trained in safety and takes over the role. In this way all Team Members develop their leadership abilities and have the opportunity to interact and coordinate with other teams. Examples:

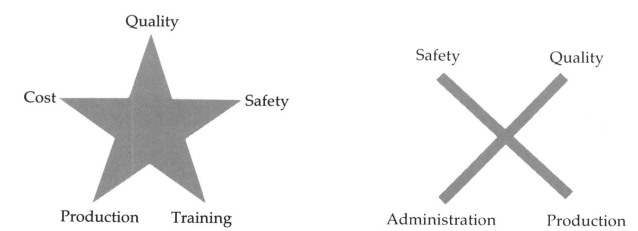

Reasons for "Shared Leadership" Among Team Members

■ The organization does not want the team to rely on just one person as the leader, but rather develop everyone's leadership abilities.

■ The organization does not want the team to revert back to the traditional way of depending on "the" leader.

■ By sharing leadership the team is not really leaderless; rather leadership shifts among team members who are responsible for various leadership functions. What these leadership duties are varies with the nature of the work, but generally team members take responsibility for leading and coordinating efforts in these areas:

• Operations	• Scheduling
• Training	• Personnel/Administration
• Safety	• Communication/Information
• Maintenance	• Quality

Each Team Member is responsible for one of these areas (some teams appoint back-up people) for a designated period of time. Along with this leadership responsibility comes:

• Training to enable Team Members to handle the responsibility

• Responsibility to attend all site meetings dealing with the area and communicate back all vital information

• Commitment to represent the team at these meetings as spokesperson.

By sharing leadership, Team Members enlarge their jobs to encompass many of the activities traditional Supervision used to do. Companies doing this are learning that training is vital to making this work. So is coordination (making the time), and rewards need to be put in place to compensate people for taking on all the extra effort required.

My Leadership Style: A Self-Assessment

Directions: Rate your present Leadership Style by indicating whether you already do this "Most Of The Time," are "Working On Doing This," or "Need To Do This."

As a Leader I: *Circle Your Answer - 1, 2, or 3*	Do This Most of the Time	Working On Doing This	Need To Do This
1. Get to know each Member of the Team.	3	2	1
2. Listen more than I talk.	3	2	1
3. Help the Team stay on target.	3	2	1
4. Remove barriers that get in the way of the Team.	3	2	1
5. Use consensus decision-making most of the time.	3	2	1
6. Make sure all Team goals have consensus.	3	2	1
7. Recognize Team Members accomplishments and give positive feedback.	3	2	1
8. Celebrate Team accomplishments.	3	2	1
9. Share information with everyone.	3	2	1
10. See mistakes as learning opportunities.	3	2	1
11. Facilitate open & honest communication.	3	2	1
12. Actively build the Team.	3	2	1
13. Coach Team Members.	3	2	1
14. Counsel Team Members.	3	2	1
15. Train Team Members.	3	2	1
16. Am open to new ways of doing things.	3	2	1
17. Encourage ideas and suggestions from Team Members and act on them.	3	2	1
18. Inform people outside our Team of what we're doing.	3	2	1
19. Facilitate the Team in identifying and solving work-related problems.	3	2	1
20. Facilitate the Team in constantly learning and changing.	3	2	1
21. Listen to our customers (internal and external).	3	2	1
22. See my behavior as role-modeling for the Team.	3	2	1
Column Total			
Grand Total of all 3 Columns			

Action Commitments:

Based on this Self-Assessment of my "Leadership Style," these are the actions I'm committed to taking:

_____

_____

_____

_____

_____

_____

_____

_____

_____

_____

_____

_____

_____

Note: My Leadership Style "Self-Assessment" could also be used to gain feedback on your leadership style from the team members. Give each member a copy and have them assess you after a specific meeting or on your general leadership. Responses should be anonymous. This can be most helpful if your attitude as the leader is that *all* feedback is good because it's valuable information you can use.

Chapter 8

Stages of Self-Directed Work Team Development

All groups go through predictable stages on their way to becoming SDWTs

Stages of Self-Directed Work Team Development **8**

As work groups engage in the process of becoming self-directed teams, they go through 3 stages. This process varies depending on the people and the organization, but generally, it takes 2-3 years before teams mature to the last stage.

The following is:

(1) A description of "What To Expect" at each of the 3 Stages.

(2) "What To Do" at each stage to keep growth and development on-going and not become "stuck."

(3) "Training Needed" at each stage.

STAGE I: Turning Crisis Into Opportunity
(lasts from start-up to 6 months)

What To Expect At Stage I:

Stage I is filled with changes. No one knows what to expect unless they've worked on a self-directed work team before and most people haven't. There is a lot of confusion, uncertainty, and frustration at the beginning. There can also be a lot of excitement. Roles are changing. Leaders are learning to be participative and give more information, decison-making power, and responsiblity to the teams. Team members have new roles that require them to be more responsible and accountable than ever before. Team members are also learning new skills and cross-training each other. Learning is frustrating—remember learning to ride a bike for the first time? Members are also learning to relate to each other in new ways. Teams require interpersonal skills like listening, communicating openly and honestly, handling meetings, etc. So, a lot of new things are happening during Stage I and as old structure (traditional work) gives way to new structure (self-directed work teams), everyone will at times feel overwhelmed, frustrated, confused, excited, challenged and energized. All of these conflicting feelings are perfectly natural.

The people who have the easiest time during Stage I are those that have faith in the philosophy of SDWTs and are personally committed to making them succeed. These are the people who look for the small successes even at this early stage and who communicate the little victories, and who praise the heroes. They don't look for the mistakes (which are inevitable) and they don't find reasons for why it will never work.

75

> Getting through Stage I requires a focus on learning, an ability to tolerate mistakes and deal with frustration, and faith that SDWTs will succeed here as they have elsewhere.

What To Do At Stage I:

■ Get to know each other. Spend time learning as much as possible about each member of the team; their likes and dislikes, strengths, weaknesses, hopes, skills, what they'd like to learn, what they're interested in, what they'd like to be doing in the future.

■ The team needs to discuss and reach agreement on its ground rules for operating, decide on its mission and goals, gather feedback, and examine its progress as a team.

■ Team Members need to agree on the kind of climate they want to create in the group and commit to building that climate together.

■ Everyone needs to have patience and faith that the team will gel and productivity, which usually dips during this start-up phase because of all the new things to be learned, will eventually rise.

■ Everyone needs to understand that trust does not develop overnight. Everyone needs to work on building trust with each other by sharing honest thoughts and feelings and developing clear expectations of each other.

■ A lot of communication is needed (talking and listening).

■ Top management needs to reassure everyone of their commitment (over-and-over) by communication and "walking-the-talk."

■ Reading, visiting sites, attending workshops /conferences are all helpful.

■ During Stage I the organization plays a key role in turning crisis into opportunity by doing the following things:

• Creating choices for people who will not work in teams. There will only be a few people who will not work in this new way and they will need to be given some choices. Usually, there are technical expertise roles that they can fill.

• Addressing the issue of job security is critical. People need to believe that gains in productivity will not cost them their job. Unless assurances like these are made, people will drag their feet, withhold ideas for improvements, and resist the change process. Job assurance does not mean a guarantee of lifetime employment, but usually takes the form of: Everyone's job will change, but no one will be out of work due to productivity gains. We will keep training you, and do everything we can to assure your work with this company.

Training Needed For Stage I:

FOR TEAM MEMBERS: Team Members will need 3 types of training -

1. **Team Training in the "New Way"** People will need training in what self-direction means, information on how this is different from traditional organizations and how everyone's role will have to change. Team Members will also need training in team skills, such as, communication (especially listening), problem-solving, decision-making, consenus, team building, group dynamics, effective meetings, conflict resolution, etc.

2. **Technical Skills Training** This will vary depending on the specific work of the team. Much of this will be done by cross-training each other so everyone becomes "multi-skilled" and able to perform each other's jobs. Often, teams also begin SPC or quality training at this time.

3. **Administrative Training** This is done very gradually over a period of years. It is best to begin with easier things such as vacation scheduling and proceed to planning, purchasing, accounting, attendance, setting standards, quality, safety, basic maintenance, and, eventually, some teams even hire and fire, and appraise each other. The correct sequence is to first give the teams information, then training, and lastly delegate the task.

FOR TEAM LEADERS: Team Leaders, Supervisors, and Managers will need training in what their new role is and how they have to behave differently in order to support teams. They will need training in all the team skills that members are trained in (communication, esp. listening, problem-solving, decision-making, consensus, team building, group dynamics, etc.) In addition, they will need training in skills such as facilitating effective team meetings, giving and receiving feedback, participative leadership, and managing change.

Management's New Role:

Management needs to fully understand this new concept and realize that unless managers behave differently, nothing will change. Management needs to give the work teams clear direction on *what* needs to be accomplished and autonomy and control over *how* they do the tasks. Teams need clear boundaries—they need to understand what they are and are not empowered to do.

STAGE II: From Dependence to Interdependence
(lasts 1 or more years)

What To Expect At Stage II:

During Stage II team members are becoming united and developing a sense of belonging. If there are designated team leaders, there is usually a reliance on them to guide the team and keep it together. The wise leader understands this and slowly gives up control to the team because only in this way will the team grow to its full capability. Decisions made by the leader must slowly be given over to the team. The team is learning to trust itself during this stage and make good decisions, and solve problems. Measurement of quality, customer service, etc. enables the team to self-correct and change its processes by tracking progress.

What To Do At Stage II:

■ As the team becomes less leader-centered and more able to make decisions and solve problems on its own, recognition and celebration of success is important to support further independence.

■ Management is learning new roles to support teams. Managers need to pull back from the day-to-day hands-on involvement and let the teams manage the work. Managers are then free to remove barriers, coordinate between teams, do long-range planning, and coach individual members.

■ People will tend to revert back to the old ways of working. This regression and dependence on leaders is natural, but leaders need to avoid the temptation to act in the old ways and give team members the support and training needed to take on more leadership, responsiblity and ownership.

■ Increase the team's knowledge of how the whole business works by supplying information and training.

■ Coordinate activities between teams and shifts that support interdependence and not negative competition.

Training Needed: At Stage II:

• Technical Skills training is still continuing. Members are cross-training each other and can now perform most of the jobs required.

• Administrative Training is still taking place. Members might at this point begin to learn interview skills for hiring new members or this might wait till Stage III.

• Interpersonal Skills training is still continuing as members strengthen their abilities to problem-solve, make decisions, make improvements, set goals, handle team meetings, deal with suppliers and customers, resolve conflicts, and coach each other.

STAGE III: Maturity & Continuous Learning

What To Expect At Stage III:

At this final stage most of the multiple technical and team skills training has taken place. The team is effective in carrying out both its task duties (the work itself) and maintenance duties (growing the team). The team members feel ownership of the team and the work, responsibility for solving problems, and have knowledge of how the whole system works. They also feel they can significantly impact the system.

Trust, respect and support among workers has developed. Time is used efficiently and problems are dealt with as they occur.

At this point tying rewards to productivity (pay for learning, profit sharing, etc.) makes sense. The SDWT is now world-class competitive, working on continuous improvement of everything. Quality and customer service should now show significant improvement over previous work systems, and members should feel more satisfaction than ever before. Since there is no end to learning, the team continually strives for improving the work and the satisfaction of individual members.

What To Do At Stage III:

■ Develop opportunities for team members to grow and develop
■ Revise systems - appraisal, reward, etc.
■ Measure, track and provide feedback so the team can self-correct
■ New goals need to be continually developed to challenge the teams (new products, new markets, new services, etc.)

■ Provide more information on total business
■ Encourage new, innovative, risky ideas
■ SDWTs should never become stagnant, but constantly find new ways to improve the work processes, the product/service (speed, cost, quality, etc.)

Training Needed At Stage III:

• Technical skills training to keep up with change
• Continuous improvement training—awareness, knowledge and skills in "Kaizen"
• At this stage some teams receive training in hiring team members and appraising each other
• Ask team members what training they want/feel they need

Questions:

Stages of SDWT Development

Step #1: Read the description of the 3 Stages.

Step #2:

a. At which stage do you believe your team is now?

_____

b. Reasons for choosing this stage?

_____

_____

_____

_____

_____

c. What do you feel the team needs to do to move to the next stage? (If you believe the team is already at Stage 3 - what do you think the team needs to do to keep growing and developing?)

_____

_____

_____

_____

_____

Step #3:
After everyone has stated their answers, discuss them as a team.

How to Keep Your Team Developing (and not get stagnant)

Teams need the following things in order to keep growing:

■ **INFORMATION** provided directly to the team on:
- Customer Requirements
- Safety
- Quality
- Finances/Business
- Goals
- Performance Measures
- SPC
- Maintenance
- Vendors/Suppliers
- Quantity
- Materials/Tools/Machines
- Cost

■ **EDUCATION/TRAINING/NEW SKILLS/KNOWLEDGE**
- Cross-training on multiple skills
- Team Skills
- Leadership/Coordinator Tasks
- Self-Directed (New ways of operating) Skills

■ **DECISION-MAKING POWER** After the necessary information has been given to the team and they've been trained properly, then everyone in the organization needs to push-down decisions that were once made by the Supervisor or Manager. This should be done gradually or the Team will feel overwhelmed and the organization will be chaotic. (Chapter 11 has more information on decision-making.)

■ **REWARDS** need to be tied to improved performance (higher quality, lower costs, more quantity, faster cycle times, new skills learned, etc.). (Chapter 14 has more information on rewards.)

TEAM EXERCISE

How to Keep Your Team Developing

1. What needed information is your team not getting at the present time?

_____

_____

_____

_____

2. What needed training is your team not getting at the present time?

_____

_____

_____

_____

3. Which decisions have been turned over to the teams?

_____

_____

_____

_____

4. Which decisions have **not** *yet been turned over?*

_____

_____

_____

_____

5. Has your reward/measurement/appraisal system been revamped to support SDWTs?

_____

_____

_____

_____

Action Commitments:

Discuss and agree on some action items to move your team forward.

_____

_____

_____

_____

_____

_____

_____

_____

_____

_____

_____

_____

_____

_____

_____

_____

Chapter 9

Effective
Team Meetings

Effective team meetings are critical to SDWTs as an opportunity to take care of important tasks and as a means of team building

Importance of Team Meetings

■ Team meetings enable teams to: solve problems, schedule work, share new ideas and suggestions, plan for the future and discuss matters relevant to everyone.

■ Team meetings also are the prime way that members experience being a team. These meetings enable team members to get to know each other better, share valuable information, make decisions together, discuss things the team is good at and what it needs to change (self-correct) in order to be more productive, more fun, and personally satisfying to the members.

■ Teams need to meet on a regular basis. Some teams meet daily (for just a few minutes), some weekly, or bi-weekly.

■ Team meetings are also a chance to practice improving one's listening skills, feedback and disclosure skills, etc.

Keep in Mind:

■ We are social animals and like to get together in teams to feel the community of other people. We need meetings to further enhance our sense of belonging and identification with our team.

■ Meetings are an opportunity to get to know other team members.

■ Meetings are an opportunity to get to support each other's ideas.

■ Meetings are an opportunity to engage in constructive conflict by disagreeing and seeking a better resolution.

■ Meetings enable the team to make decisions together.

■ Meetings enable the team to solve problems and be creative together.

■ Meetings can be fun.

■ Meetings are a time to quickly share information that everyone needs to know.

■ Meetings are a great way to get everyone involved, committed, and responsible for things that need getting done.

■ Size of the meeting: If you get much above 12 people it will be difficult to get a lot accomplished. Keep the number limited to all team members plus a few guests *if* they are essential.

■ A facilitator, (team leader or member who acts as team leader) when properly trained, can help the team accomplish its objectives. The facilitator must understand his/her role is to help the team be effective by keeping the team on task, quieting the talkative, drawing out the silent, keeping conflict constructive, keeping the group aware of its process (how it does things), clarifying, moving discussion forward, and reaching resolution. Some teams appoint the same facilitator for all their meetings, and others rotate the role among all the members.

Team Meeting Assessment

Answer the following questions about your team's meetings. Rate your meetings on a scale from 0 (Never) to 4 (Always). *Circle your answer.*

	Never	Seldom	Usually	Frequently	Always
1. Everyone understands the purpose of the meeting.	0	1	2	3	4
2. Everyone is involved in the decision-making process.	0	1	2	3	4
3. Everyone is committed to the team's decisions.	0	1	2	3	4
4. Everyone speaks at our meetings. No one person dominates.	0	1	2	3	4
5. The entire team attends.	0	1	2	3	4
6. We have a stated agenda prepared ahead of time with everyone's input.	0	1	2	3	4
7. We carefully plan the order of the agenda, placing the most important items first.	0	1	2	3	4
8. We make sure the meetings are short. (Never more than 2 hours)	0	1	2	3	4
9. We meet on a regular basis. (daily, weekly, bi-weekly, etc.)	0	1	2	3	4
10. We circulate background information or proposal papers before each meeting (and provide short summaries of very long papers).	0	1	2	3	4
Total:					

	Never	Seldom	Usually	Frequently	Always
11. We have a meeting facilitator (either the same person or the role shifts among members) to guide the team meeting process.	0	1	2	3	4
12. The facilitator restricts his/her interventions to a minimum (listens more than talks).	0	1	2	3	4
13. Everyone listens to each other.	0	1	2	3	4
14. Everyone paraphrases to make sure they understand.	0	1	2	3	4
15. The facilitator moves the discussion forward when the team gets bogged down or off track.	0	1	2	3	4
16. Everyone understands and accepts resolutions made by the team.	0	1	2	3	4
17. Team members are given feedback when they delay or divert the team's progress in discussion, problem-solving, etc.	0	1	2	3	4
18. The team is able to reach consensus in decision-making.	0	1	2	3	4
19. The team is able to resolve issues.	0	1	2	3	4
20. Team members seek clarification if they need it.	0	1	2	3	4
21. The atmosphere in the meeting is relaxed, comfortable and informal.	0	1	2	3	4
Total:					

	Never	Seldom	Usually	Frequently	Always
22. Discussion is closed when it's clear a resolution has been reached.	0	1	2	3	4
23. Decisions are not postponed simply because they're difficult.	0	1	2	3	4
24. Before the end of the meeting the Facilitator gives:					
■ A brief clear summary of what has been agreed on	0	1	2	3	4
■ Members are asked to confirm the actions they've committed to	0	1	2	3	4
■ A time and place are set for the next meeting.	0	1	2	3	4
25. Minutes of the meeting are recorded and distributed to members, leaders, support people, etc.	0	1	2	3	4

Total					
Total of All Columns					
Grand Total					

(A Perfect Score is 108.)

TEAM EXERCISE

Effective Team Meetings

When everyone is finished with the "Team Meeting Assessment," discuss answers with the entire Team:

■ What do Team Members see as some strengths about your team meetings?

_____

_____

_____

_____

_____

_____

_____

■ What are some areas the Team needs to improve? (Make a list of all the suggestions for improvements.)

_____

_____

_____

_____

_____

_____

_____

Action Commitments:

Discuss and agree on actions the team feels need to be taken at this time to make Team Meetings more effective.

_____

_____

_____

_____

_____

_____

_____

_____

_____

_____

_____

_____

_____

_____

_____

_____

_____

_____

_____

_____

_____

_____

Chapter 10

Communication:
Listening & Information Sharing

SDWTs require a high-degree of communication; how people listen to each other and share information is critical

Self-directed work teams require a high-degree of communication between team members, the team and the leader (whether leadership is fixed or rotates), the team and other teams, shifts, and with support people (management, other departments, etc.).

For some people this high degree of communication will be fairly easy, and for others it will be very difficult. As individuals, we all differ in our communication style, but all of us can improve the *quality* of our communication.

Since communication is such a broad topic that can mean so many things, we want to focus on two aspects of communication we feel are critical to SDWTs: Listening Skills and Information-Sharing.

PART I: Listening Skills

Let's start by looking at your listening skills. Please fill out this questionnaire.

Listening Questionnaire

1. How would you describe yourself as a listener at work?

   _____

   _____

   _____

2. How would you describe yourself as a listener at home?

   _____

   _____

   _____

3. How would the following people rate *you* as a listener? Explain.

	Poor Listener	Average Listener	Good Listener	Excellent Listener
Your Team Leader?	1	2	3	4

Explanation _____

_____

Other Team Members?	1	2	3	4

Explanation _____

_____

Customers?	1	2	3	4

Explanation _____

_____

Your Spouse? (if applicable)	1	2	3	4

Explanation _____

One of Your Children? (if applicable)	1	2	3	4

Explanation _____

Your Best Friend?	1	2	3	4

Explanation _____

4. What conclusions do you draw from your answers?

_____

_____

_____

_____

Why Listening is the #1 Skill of an Effective Team Member

If you think your listening could use some improvement, you have a lot of company—most people are poor listeners. This has been borne out by standardized tests that have found people only hear about 25% of the message and by the intangible evidence all around us that good listeners are rare indeed.

We think listening is the single most important communication skill a team member or leader must possess. If you want proof of this, think for a moment of the last time someone really listened to you. It may have been recently or a while ago. Try to remember how you felt.

Most people say they felt some or all of the following:

- they mattered as a person
- they were important
- they were worth the time spent on listening to them
- they had ideas, resources that were valuable
- they felt empowered

Listening to people increases their level of self-esteem and, therefore, they are more likely to:

- offer suggestions
- offer ideas
- take risks
- speak openly
- get involved
- bring problems to light
- discuss their honest feelings
- be creative

All of these actions are key to bringing about the kind of employee involvement Self-Directed Work Teams are all about.

What Does A "Good Listener" Do?

**Think of the "best listener" you know. What does he/she do?
List all answers here:**

_____   _____

_____   _____

_____   _____

_____   _____

_____   _____

"Active" Listening

The psychologist Carl Rogers called what good listeners do—
ACTIVE LISTENING—because it's not a passive activity.

The Active Listener is:
■ Listening for feelings as well as facts
■ Making eye contact
■ Paraphrasing back to the speaker what the listener heard (to make sure what he/she heard was what the speaker meant)
■ Creating an atmosphere for listening

The Active Listener also chooses NOT to:
■ Make judgements about what he/she is hearing because this will shut down communication. (People want to be understood, not judged.)
■ Mentally rehearse what he/she is going to say next
■ Do anything else while he/she is listening
■ Interrupt or complete sentences
■ Assume he/she already knows what the speaker is going to say
■ Offer advice or solutions. Rather assumes the speaker can arrive at his/her own solutions

---

The Importance of Listening
When Leading/Facilitating a Team

Effective leaders/facilitators listen to individuals and to the group as a whole. They constantly pay attention to what is happening in the group and ask themselves:

■ Where is this group in terms of its development? (Are people still getting to know each other, building trust, etc?)

■ What is the energy level of the group right now? (high? low?)

■ What feelings (conscious and unconscious) are being expressed today? (frustration? anger?)

■ What does this team need? (more fun? some success? questions answered? more structure? more agreement? more conflict? a "clearing-of-the-air" session? problem-solving?)

Listening And Values

In order to really listen to others effectively, one has to have a certain value-base because Active Listening is more than just skills. If it is not connected to a deep-rooted set of beliefs and values, it is just a "technique" and people will feel manipulated rather than listened to.

So, what are these deeply held beliefs/values?

1. BELIEVING THAT LISTENING TO PEOPLE IS IMPORTANT AND WORTH TAKING THE TIME. Have you ever wondered why some people take the time to listen and others never have the time? Good listeners believe listening is important and worth the time it takes and the evidence is that they're right. People who listen are more effective. They know the real problems and concerns of others because people trust them, want to talk with them, and work with them.

2. BEING "OTHER-PERSON" FOCUSED. Believing that other people are important and have ideas, points-of-view, solutions to problems, etc. Letting the speaker control the conversation and not redirecting the focus.

3. BELIEVING FEELINGS ARE AS IMPORTANT AS FACTS. Listening between the words for what is not said, for tone of voice, paying attention to body language, etc.

4. BELIEVING LISTENING IS POWERFUL AND EMPOWERING. Building another person's self-esteem by really listening to them, understanding them, and making them feel valued, cared for and important.

5. BELIEVING THAT PEOPLE ARE CAPABLE OF SOLVING THEIR OWN PROBLEMS. Listening to people does not mean solving their problems for them. In fact, most of the time we want people to understand us without "telling us" what we "should" do.

6. BELIEVING THAT EMPATHY IS IMPORTANT. Listening to people enables us to appreciate what it's like to "walk in their shoes" and see things from their point of view.

7. BELIEVING EVERYONE HAS SOMETHING VALUABLE TO SAY. Not just listening to "important" people, but listening to everyone.

Notes:

TEAM EXERCISE

Group Practice Session in Paraphrasing

Step #1: Ask the Team to define "Paraphrasing."*

Step #2: Ask a volunteer from the team to talk for a minute or 2 about anything at all (a hobby, an interest, a pet peeve, etc.); everyone else will listen. When they're finished everyone is going to paraphrase what the speaker said—both the meaning and the feelings. No one person will paraphrase all of it; just some part. They will address the speaker and ask the speaker if their paraphrase is correct because only the speaker knows for sure what he/she meant.

(Facilitator: Make sure people are really paraphrasing. If you think they're doing something else—asking questions, making comments, adding personal information—ask them if they are paraphrasing. Try to develop in the team members an awareness of what paraphrasing really is and what it isn't.)

Step #3: As a summary, ask the team what this demonstration of Active Listening illustrates. Typical answers might be:
- "How much meaning and feeling there is in just a few minutes of talk, if we really listened."
- "I completely missed that part —but someone else heard it."

Step #4. Lastly, ask the Team to summarize the main points about Active Listening.

---

*Definition of Paraphrasing:
Repeating back to the speaker what you, the listener, heard them say (either facts or feelings) and checking out the accuracy of your listening. It's not parroting (repeating what you heard word-for-word because that's not really listening—that's what they said, not necessarily what you heard). It's not asking questions because that is focusing on what *you* want to know, and it takes control away from the speaker. And it's definitely not telling the speaker about a similar experience you had.

Active Listening is:

- Listening for words and feelings
- Paraphrasing
- Being other-person centered
- *Active* not passive
- Not giving solutions, but allowing the speaker to talk through the problem and reach their own conclusions
- A way of really understanding another person
- Non-judgmental; an attitude of acceptance
- Building the self-esteem and importance of the human being
- Empowering
- Connected to values and not just a *technique*
- Powerful—that's why we even pay people (psychiatrists, counselors, etc.) to really hear us

Listening Self-Assessment

Indicate with a check (✔) how you feel you are presently doing in each skill area. Choose one.

Skill Areas:	Having Difficulty	Doing Alright But Need Developing	Skill I'm Good At
Listening for Facts			
Listening to My Own Feelings			
Listening for the Other Person's Feelings			
Paraphrasing			
Expressing My Feelings			
Asking Open-ended Questions (ones that require more than "yes" or "no" answers)			
Being Non-Judgmental (Open-minded)			
Not Interrupting			
Willing to Confront Conflict			
Remembering Information			
Not Completing Other's Sentences			
Not Giving Advice			
Helping Other Person Hear Themselves			
Helping the Other Person Solve Their Own Problems			
Making Eye Contact			
Observing Body Language			
Comfortable with Silence			
Other-Person Focused			
Taking Notes for Retention			
Not Getting Defensive			
Establishing Trust			
Encouraging Feedback			
Not Evaluating			
Not Thinking of What I'm Going to Say Next			

Questions:

1. The strengths I have as a listener are: _____

_____

_____

_____

_____

_____

_____

2. Some things I do that get in the way of active listening are: _____

_____

_____

_____

_____

_____

_____

3. I want to become a better listener in order to: _____

_____

_____

_____

_____

_____

_____

Action Commitments:

■ To become a better listener I need to:

a. Do More _____

_____

_____

_____

_____

b. Do Less _____

_____

_____

_____

_____

c. Stop Doing _____

_____

_____

_____

_____

d. Start Doing _____

_____

_____

_____

_____

■ I'll know I'm a better listener when _____

_____

_____

_____

_____

_____

PART II: Information-Sharing: Disclosure

The second aspect of communication we want to focus on is Information-Sharing: the information we disclose to others and the feedback we receive from others.

Teamwork requires a high degree of information-sharing. It is important for the team to know these things about each other in order to work effectively:

- Strengths and weaknesses
- Talents
- Interests
- Likes and dislikes
- What people want to learn
- What people want in their career
- Problems
- Solutions or suggestions
- New ideas for improvements, products, services, etc.
- Feelings about each other
- What help people need
- What turns others on (motivates them)
- What turns others off
- Hot buttons
- What people are trying to change about themselves (quit smoking, control anger, etc.)
- Something about each other's lives outside of work
- Concerns or worries
- What new things others are trying to learn

The team needs to work at creating an environment where people will feel secure and safe enough to discuss these things to the degree they feel comfortable.

TEAM EXERCISE
Disclosure Pairings

Team members need to get to know one another before they can develop trust and work together effectively. People differ in how much they disclose about themselves.

Some people disclose almost nothing and others perceive them as remote, distant, unknown, etc. Some people talk only about themselves and seem not to be interested or concerned with anyone else. Ideally, we want to create a balance by disclosing information about ourselves and also listening actively to others.

Instructions:
- Ask everyone to pair with the person in the group they know "least well." (If there is an uneven number of people, there will be one triad.)

- After everyone is sitting with a partner, use the following questions to engage in a dialogue.

- Take turns choosing a question from the list you want to talk about. Take about 30 minutes - going back-and-forth, each taking turns disclosing something about yourself and listening to your partner.

Questions: *(Choose any of them - You don't have to go in order.)*

1. What was the most interesting period of your life?
2. What has been the most difficult period?
3. How do you happen to be doing the work you're presently doing?
4. What things do you do very well?
5. What are some things you want to stop doing?
6. What are some things you're learning right now?
7. What are your favorite things to do?
8. What are some experiences you're looking forward to having in the future?
9. What's the best team experience you've ever had?
10. Tell about a missed opportunity.

11. What are some things you want to start doing at this point in your life?
12. What are some values you're very committed to?
13. What's an issue you feel strongly about?
14. What are some things you'd really like to get better at?
15. Talk about something you successfully changed.
16. Talk about a turning point in your life.
17. Discuss an important person in your life.
18. Talk about an important event.
19. How do you feel about your life right now?
20. How do you envision your life 10 years from now?

Information-Sharing: Feedback

The feedback we receive from others is the second element of information-sharing.

There are two ways to get feedback from others: Asking for it or receiving unsolicited feedback. If you have an open, honest, trusting relationship with another person, like a best friend, chances are he/she gives you feedback whether or not you ask for it. Since it is honest, it is very helpful (even when you don't want to hear it).

When we need feedback but are unlikely to get it because someone doesn't know us or trust us, we have to ask for it. Anytime we want information on our effect on others, we can ask.

Since Team Members of SDWTs are interdependent on each other to carry out their work, it is very important for Team Members to give open and honest feedback about how their actions affect the work of the team. This requires a degree of honesty about matters that we have not traditionally been open about at work. (Examples might be: tardiness, absenteeism, scheduling issues (covering for each other), quality issues, mistakes, accomplishments, problems, etc.). This is why it is so important for a team to discuss, agree on, and establish ground rules and shared norms for conduct. But these are only effective if people are open and honest with each other.

Many self-directed work teams conduct peer appraisals. Traditional, one-way, boss-subordinate appraisals have never worked very well since many people feel judged and not helped. The case for peer appraisal says that people who work together know each other best, know the quality of each other's work, and know the extent to which each member affects the entire team. And this is all true in effective teams. (More on Peer Review in Chapter 16.)

Tips On Feedback:

■ The best feedback is specific not vague. (Ex. "When I said..., did you think...? or "When I ..., what did you feel?")

■ Listen to the feedback without getting defensive.

■ Do not blindly accept feedback as the ultimate truth. Let it in and give yourself some time to think about it.

■ Paraphrase the feedback to be sure you really understand what the other person is saying.

■ Remember: all feedback is "good" because it gives you valuable information about how others think and feel about your actions.

TEAM EXERCISE

Positive Feedback Sharing:

Many people think "feedback" means criticism, but we are also talking about positive feedback. In fact, we think that most of the time it is more rewarding, more effective, and definitely more fun, to share the positive so people can build on their strengths. Most people feel that they do not get enough positive strokes, yet they are reluctant to give "too much praise." We think this is unfortunate. Let's start "catching people doing something right."

Instructions:

• Pair up with the person on your team you know best. Exchange books with them.
• Place their name at the top of the "POSITIVE FEEDBACK" form on the back of this page and your name at the bottom.
• Now, thinking of them, fill in the 15 "TOPIC ITEMS" listed. (Be as specific as you can, skip items you have no information on, and, most importantly, be sincere.)
• When you're both finished, exchange papers.
• Discuss, ask questions, give reactions, etc. to the positive feedback you just received.
• After every pair has talked for about 15 minutes, ask everyone for some reactions to the exercise. (Total Time: 30 min.)

Use "Positive Feedback Form" on next page.

Positive Feedback

For _____
Name

TOPIC ITEMS:	Positive Feedback - Comments, Examples, Reactions & Impressions
1. Communications Skills:	
2. Creativity:	
3. Decision-making:	
4. Problem-solving:	
5. Membership Skills:	
6. Leadership Qualities:	
7. Experience/Knowledge/Expertise:	
8. Accomplishments:	
9. Interpersonal Skills:	
10. Technical Skills:	
11. Motivation/Commitment:	
12. Cooperation/Collaboration:	
13. Willingness to Take Risks:	
14. Learning/Growing:	
15. Contributions to Team:	

From _____
Name

Chapter **11**

Understanding Group Dynamics

Assessments for developing
awareness, knowledge & skills
in group behavior

Towards the end of a team meeting, ask everyone to answer the following questions about the meeting that just took place: (Explain that the purpose of this is to raise everyone's awareness level of group dynamics.)

Group Dynamics Assessment

Directions: Read each question and choose the answer that best describes this group. Circle the letter corresponding to the description on the accompanying "Answer Sheet" on the next page.

After observing the meeting we just had, what is your opinion on these 10 dynamics:

1. Was the group tense or at ease?
   A. Tense, uncomfortable, insecure
   B. A little uncomfortable
   C. About average
   D. Comfortable, relaxed, at ease

2. How clear were the group's goals? Were all efforts directed toward a common focus?
   A. No apparent group goal; members uncertain or in conflict with each other; efforts going in more than one direction
   B. Some confusion, some conflict
   C. Average goal clarity
   D. Goal(s) discussed, all members understood and accepted the group's goal(s) and directed efforts toward a common focus

3. How involved/participative was the group in doing the task?
   A. Uninterested; wasting time; bored
   B. Less interested than usual
   C. Usual, average level of interest
   D. Involved, interested, concerned

4. How much trust between the members of the group? How freely and honestly were feelings and ideas expressed?
   A. Little trust, much defensiveness, reserve and caution
   B. Some guardedness, considerable restraint in what was said
   C. Trust among most, not all members
   D. Complete trust, open & honest expression of thoughts, feelings, ideas, and problems

5. How focused was the group on the task, the present tense, and happenings related to the group?
   A. Completely "there-and-then" focused on topics not relevant to the task and past experiences
   B. More related to experiences outside the group or the present, but some discussion of what is happening now
   C. Most of time spent on tasks and happenings relevant to the present task
   D. Completely here-and-now, focused on tasks and happenings in the group

6. How were leadership needs met?
   A. Leadership needs were not met—group drifted, floundered, lacked coordination
   B. Leadership needs met only occasionally when one or two stronger members took charge for brief periods
   C. Effective leader and some leadership by several members, little dependency or counter-dependency
   D. Leadership role distributed among members, shifting as the situation changed

7. How were decisions handled?
   A. Group could not reach any decisions
   B. Decisions made by dominance of one person
   C. Decisions made by a few people with silence interpreted as consent
   D. Decisions made by consensus with dissenting opinions heard and incorporated into final compromise that all supported

8. How much of the group's resources were used and how was conflict dealt with?
   A. A few people contributed; those who differed were squelched or ignored; many did not contribute
   B. About average; some contributed, differences smoothed over and not explored
   C. Most contributed; differences and disagreements examined
   D. Everyone participated; differences and disagreements creatively used

9. How strong are feelings of belonging in the group? Closeness? Loyalty?
   A. Group members do not care about each other
   B. Group members are friendly with some members, but not all
   C. Most members feel sense of belonging, closeness and loyalty
   D. Strong sense of belonging, closeness and loyalty on the part of all team members

10. How growth-oriented, experimental, and learning-centered is the group?
    A. Very little commitment to learning
    B. Some evidence of desire to learn new things, but most in favor of same old ways
    C. Many indications of desire to learn; asking questions, seeking new possibilities
    D. Constantly learning and seeking new ways, new ideas, and creative approaches

Group Dynamics Assessment

Answer Sheet:

Circle the letter corresponding to your choice of descriptions.

(1.)   A   B   C   D

(2.)   A   B   C   D

(3.)   A   B   C   D

(4.)   A   B   C   D

(5.)   A   B   C   D

(6.)   A   B   C   D

(7.)   A   B   C   D

(8.)   A   B   C   D

(9.)   A   B   C   D

(10.)   A   B   C   D

Understanding Group Dynamics

As a facilitator or team member you want your team to move from scoring "A" on the assessment to scoring "D."

In other words you want your group to understand group dynamics and develop into a team that is:

- Comfortable with each other (not tense)
- Clear about goals
- Committed to goals
- Totally (100%) involved and participating
- Trusting
- Focused on the present
- Developing leadership in everyone
- Able to make good decisions (with quality & commitment)
- Loyal
- Constantly growing and learning

Teams are developed by helping each team member become more aware of the dynamics taking place in the group. The assessment you just took can be taken periodically to see if the team is moving closer to the "D" range.

Notes:

Actions to Facilitate "Positive" Dynamics

A Team Member or Facilitator can be very helpful in moving a Team forward by doing the following things:

1. Paying attention to what is said, not said, the mood of the group, the energy level, body language.

2. Constantly asking yourself: "What does this group need?"

3. Role modeling Active Listening (paraphrasing, speaking less than listening, listening for feelings, etc.)

4. Helping people get to know each other (building trust).

5. Making sure the atmosphere is relaxed, comfortable, and free of fear.

6. Making sure everyone has an opportunity to participate.

7. Keeping the group focused by making them aware when they get off task and guiding them back.

8. Encouraging open and honest expression of ideas.

9. Not suppressing conflict, but keeping it focused on the problem not the personalities.

10. Providing structure for the group (but not too much or people will feel you're trying to control them).

11. Investing leadership in everyone so as not to create dependency on one person.

12. Helping individuals balance their personal needs with the team's needs.

13. Providing group with feedback to recognize its achievements and correct problems.

14. Helping the group set ground rules, make effective decisions, form goals, and measure itself.

15. Focusing on the process: How information is gathered, how decisions are made, how problems are solved or delayed, etc.

16. Designing the physical layout to be conducive to people feeling comfortable and relaxed, able to see each other, all equal, etc.

17. Making sure the organization context supports the team: Offers clear goals, a reward system based on recognizing performance, etc.

18. Coaching and assisting team members.

19. Helping people develop their team skills.

20. Helping team members understand the consequences of their behavior by providing honest, timely feedback.

The following exercise was designed to help raise everyone's awareness of and sensitivity to the team's climate:

Team Climate Survey

Instructions: Circle the number on the scale indicating the degree to which the attribute characterizes this team now.

	Low Degree				Average Degree				High Degree		
1. Commitment to task?	0	1	2	3	4	5	6	7	8	9	10
2. Openness to learning?	0	1	2	3	4	5	6	7	8	9	10
3. Candor & honesty?	0	1	2	3	4	5	6	7	8	9	10
4. Attentive listening for understanding?	0	1	2	3	4	5	6	7	8	9	10
5. Willingness to confront differences in ideas?	0	1	2	3	4	5	6	7	8	9	10
6. Too polite; smoothing over differences; unwilling to deal with conflict?	0	1	2	3	4	5	6	7	8	9	10
7. Defensiveness or lack of trust?	0	1	2	3	4	5	6	7	8	9	10
8. Creative; willing to take risks and try new things?	0	1	2	3	4	5	6	7	8	9	10
9. Attempts to dominate?	0	1	2	3	4	5	6	7	8	9	10
10. Cutting off people?	0	1	2	3	4	5	6	7	8	9	10
11. Participation from everyone?	0	1	2	3	4	5	6	7	8	9	10
12. Consideration of others?	0	1	2	3	4	5	6	7	8	9	10
13. Expression of feelings?	0	1	2	3	4	5	6	7	8	9	10
14. Paraphrasing?	0	1	2	3	4	5	6	7	8	9	10
15. Relaxed; free of tension?	0	1	2	3	4	5	6	7	8	9	10
16. Leader supported by team?	0	1	2	3	4	5	6	7	8	9	10
17. Conviction to stand up for honestly held views?	0	1	2	3	4	5	6	7	8	9	10
18. Interest in one another as people?	0	1	2	3	4	5	6	7	8	9	10

Climate Survey Discussion

■ Ask everyone in the group to complete the "Team Climate Survey." When everyone is finished, ask people to raise their hands as you call out the numbers. For example: "Would you please raise your hand if you scored the group 0-3 on Question #1 Commitment to task?" "4-5-6 or 7?" "8-9 or 10?"

■ After the entire list has been gone through, open this up for group discussion by asking: "What questions or comments do you have now that you've seen how everyone answered their survey?"

■ This exercise can be done periodically by the team to see if dynamics have changed or improved. It will give everyone an idea of how people see the group, what people want to change, or what they like about the group.

───────────── ★ ─────────────

Action Commitments:

What actions is our team commited to taking to continue to improve our climate?

_____

_____

_____

_____

_____

_____

_____

_____

_____

_____

_____

_____

_____

_____

Chapter **12**

Decision-Making

Types of decision-making, achieving SYNERGY, and the criteria for a "good" decision

Can a team of people working together make better decisions than any individual member would on their own? Let's test this out with the following* team exercise:

The Ingredients of a "Good" Marriage: A Decision-Making Exercise

In a poll** conducted in December of 1985 by the Los Angeles Times, 2,308 adults were asked what ingredients they thought made for a good marriage.

Step #1:

As an individual, please rank order these 10 ingredients. Rank as #1 the ingredient you believe the adults in this poll mentioned more often than any other. Rank as #2 the second most frequently sited ingredient, and so on for all 10 items. #10 should be the one mentioned least by the adults polled. Place your rankings in the first column of the Answer Sheet "Step #1 - Individual Ranking."

Items:	Step #1 Individual Ranking	Step #2 Team's Ranking	Step #3 Correct Ranking	Step #4 Difference Between Steps 1 & 3	Step #5 Difference Between Steps 2 & 3
Financial security					
Being able to keep romance alive					
Being in love					
Having similar ideas on how to handle money					
Having the same kinds of life-activities and friends					
Being able to talk about your feelings					
Spousal sexual fidelity					
Being able to see the humorous side of things					
Having similar ideas on child rearing					
Having a good sexual relationship					
Source: *Inside America*, Louis Harris			**Totals:**		
*If your team has more than 8 members, you can do this exercise as two teams.				Individual Score	Team Score

121

Step #2:

Hold on to your individual rankings and now as a team reach consensus* on the rankings of the items. (Take 30 min.) Place your "Team Rankings" in second column, "Step 2". *See page 37 for "Guidelines For Reaching Consensus."

The Decision-Making "Process"

Before going on to "Step 3," spend a few minutes looking at the *process* by which your team produced their results.

Instructions: Answer the following questions about the decision-making exercise your team just had:

Circle your answer on the scale of 1-5 according to how you feel.

1. How listened to did you feel?
1	2	3	4	5
Not at all				Completely

2. How much influence did you feel you exerted on the team's decision?
1	2	3	4	5
None at all				A Great Deal

3. How satisfied do you feel about the final decisions made by the team?
1	2	3	4	5
Not at all				Completely

4. How responsible do you feel for the team's decision?
1	2	3	4	5
Not at all				Completely

5. How committed do you feel to the team's decision?
1	2	3	4	5
Not at all				Completely

6. As you think back on it, is there anything you think the team should have done but didn't or something the team should do differently next time?

_____

_____

> When everyone has finished, discuss your answers with the entire team. (15 min.)

Step #3:

On the bottom of page 126 are listed the correct rankings according to the poll. Write these rankings in the column marked "Correct Ranking - Step #3" on page 121.

Step #4

Ask each member to subtract their "Individual Ranking" - Step #1 from the "Correct Ranking" - Step #3. (plus or minus doesn't matter). If there is *no* difference between the Individual and the Team Ranking, place a zero in the column for that item. After you've subtracted each of the 10 items, total the column to give yourself an "Individual Score."

Step #5:

Subtract the "Team Rankings" - Step #2 from the "Correct Ranking" - Step #3 (plus or minus doesn't matter). Place these numbers in the column marked "Step #5" and total this column for a "Team Score."

Analyzing Your Team Results:

		Team 1	Team 2
Step #6	**Average Individual Score:** Add together *all* the individual scores and divide by the number of people in the team		
Step #7	**Lowest Individual Score**		
Step #8	**Team Score** from Step #5		
Step #9	**Gain or Loss Score:** Difference between Team Score (Step #8) and Average Individual Score (Step #6)		
Step #10	**Gain or Loss Score:** Difference between Team Score (Step #8) and Lowest Individual Score (Step #7)		

Did Your Team Achieve Synergy - Yes? No? (Circle One)

If your "Team Score" is better than your "Average Individual Score" your team achieved synergy. If your "Team Score" is better than even the "Lowest Indiviual Score," then your synergy was even greater! (Achieving both of these is less common than achieving just the first one, so give yourself a lot of credit if you were able to do this.)

Synergy is defined as the whole being greater than the sum of the parts. In other words, team members put their heads together and make decisions that are better than anyone could have made on their own. This is the payoff of teamwork—accomplishing things together that we couldn't do on our own.

Conditions for Synergy:

- Team Members that know and trust each other.

- A relaxed, comfortable atmosphere.

- Sufficient time.

- Diversity respected and seen as an advantage.

- Conflict seen as healthy.

- Listening to each other.

- Willingness to compromise.

- New, creative ideas supported.

- No one person dominates the team. Total participation. Decisions not made until everyone is heard from.

- Open and honest communication.

- Sharing all relevant information. Freedom to exert influence and take risks without fear of ridicule.

- The team continually examines its processes and self-corrects (learns from experience and makes changes).

TEAM EXERCISE

Synergy

Spend a few minutes creating a joint list of why you think the team *was* able or was *not* able to achieve synergy.

_____

_____

_____

_____

_____

_____

_____

_____

_____

_____

_____

_____

_____

_____

_____

_____

_____

Correct Rankings:

Financial security (10), Being able to keep romance alive (4), Being in love (1), Have similar ideas on how to handle money (8), Having the same kinds of life activities & friends (9), Being able to talk about your feelings (2), Spousal sexual fidelity (3), Being able to see the humorous side of things (5), Having similar ideas on child-rearing (7), Having a good sexual relationship (6).

SDWTs and Decision-Making Styles:

To see why Self-Directed Work Teams have an advantage in the area of decision-making, let's look at 3 styles of decision-making and the pluses and minuses of each style:

Style #1: Directive
One person with authority makes the decision for everyone.

This has been the most prevelant style in traditional organizations. The boss makes the decisions for everyone. The chief advantage is speed and in times of crisis or emergency this may be the best style. When speed is called for to avert a disaster, one person with authority has to make a decision quickly.

But the disadvantages of this style are so numerous that we are seeing it used less-and-less. Here are just some of the disadvantages:

■ Only one person's wisdom, facts, knowledge, expertise, etc. is being used. (The people who may know the most about it are not being consulted.)

■ Others may not agree with the decision and will not carry it out.

■ People will feel left out of the decision-making process and may not feel committed to the decision or responsible for making it succeed.

■ There is no opportunity for group synergy.

■ The how and why of the decision may not be readily apparent.

Style #2: Consultative
One person with authority makes the decision for everyone but only after consulting with everyone.

Style #2 is not as fast as Style #1 but now more knowledge, wisdom, ideas from other people are being tapped so the possibility of a better quality decision exists. Commitment to carry out the decision might also be greater since now people are being asked for input and feel more involved. Nevertheless, only one person with authority will make the final decision. Many leaders believe this style is participative, but it is only so in a very limited way.

Style #3: Participative
The whole team decides together how to solve a problem, schedule work, plan and prioritize, set goals and objectives, make buying decisions, etc.

This style is most prevelant in self-directed work teams where underlying assumptions are that:

1. Everyone has some valuable knowledge to contribute, so putting "our heads together" will produce higher quality results.

2. The commitment of the people involved is essential for making the decision succeed.

3. The team together can be more creative—synergistic than people working alone.

4. Decision-making is an opportunity to build the team.

5. Empowerment and self-direction really means being able to make decisions.

6. The people doing the work are the best experts on the work.

7. The team by concentrating on the planning, scheduling, performing, checking and improving the work can free leaders to do more cross-functional work, concentrate on providing resources, do more coaching of individual members, and focus on long-term planning. Turning decision-making over to the team enables leaders to do the real job of leadership and let team members manage the work.

———————— ★ ————————

Delegating *Not* Dumping:

Participative decision-making has great potential provided the team is properly prepared in the following ways:

■ The team is given the information it needs
■ The team is given the proper training in decision-making, problem-solving, interpersonal skills (communication, listening, etc.).

There is risk involved in this style. The team may not make the best decision (especially a new team or one that has not been accustomed to making decisions together). The worst thing a leader can do is reverse a decision once he/she has handed it over because this will hurt his/her credibility. So, a wise leader makes the first decision-making activities as risk-free as possible by handing over easy decisions first.

It helps to remember that the job of leadership is to set direction by stating goals or tasks and then a wise leader gives the team the autonomy to perform the task as they see fit. As long as the team members believe they have chosen the best way, it may be the best way for them, even though it is not how the leader would do it.

Decision-Making & Empowerment

How decisions are made is critical to organizations. Real power is the ability to make decisions. All three styles of decision-making are needed in organizations. But we have traditionally over used style #1-Directive and underused Style #3-Participative. SDWTs are successful because decisions are made at all levels of the organization. And the people who know the work best are given the power to put their knowledge, skills, talents, ideas, and suggestions into practice.

Criteria For A "Good" Decision:

A good decision has two components: **Quality and Commitment.** A *Quality* decision takes into account the relevant facts and makes good use of those facts. It is a logical decision with good, sound reasoning behind it.

The second element of a good decision is that in addition to having quality, it also has the *Commitment* of the people who will carry it out.

A good decision that has quality, but does not have the commitment of people, is useless because no one will carry it out and make it succeed. On the other hand, a poor quality decision that everyone acts on is equally wasteful and destructive.

Both Quality and Commitment are critical to effective decision-making. It is in this area that Self-Directed Work Teams have their greatest advantage. When teams are provided with the right information, training, and the power to make decisions, they can produce high-quality and high-commitment decisions.

What Kinds of Decisions Do Self-Directed Teams Make?

The whole idea behind SDWTs is that the people closest to the work make decisions on planning, executing and improving the work. Therefore, SDWTs make a lot of decisions only supervisors and managers used to make, such as:

- ☐ Vacation scheduling

- ☐ Who does what on a given day

- ☐ Solving problems of all types

- ☐ Making improvements on: How the work is done, the quality of the product, the customer service

- ☐ Safety

- ☐ Housekeeping

- ☐ Making minor repairs and performing routine maintenance

- ☐ Setting goals

- ☐ Stopping the work in order to address quality problems

- ☐ Working with customers (internal & external), suppliers, vendors

- ☐ Peer assessments

- ☐ Hiring & firing work team members

- ☐ Managing budgets

- ☐ Assessing & addressing training needs

- ☐ Measuring performance of individuals and the team

- ☐ Making compensation decisions

- ☐ Deciding which team member gets a limited resource

★

Empowering SDWTs

SDWTs are empowered by increasing their ability to make decisions. Several factors need to be taken into consideration: the nature of the work, the culture of the organization, contract agreements with unions, and the skill development of the team members. The key is what makes sense in terms of the nature of the work (and all situations are unique) and what makes sense to the people (and all people

are unique). It is best with a new team to begin with the easier items, such as vacation scheduling and keep adding new decisions after people have the necessary information and training in the administrative, technical, and interpersonal skills necessary.

Some teams never hire new members; those that do, only do this after they have been operating for a while (probably a year at the very least). A team keeps growing and developing by being given more information, training, knowledge and skills, and power—and power in organizations is making decisions.

TEAM EXERCISE

Decision-Making

Instructions: Step #1: Place a check (✔) in the boxes on the previous page to indicate which decisions your team is making now.

Step #2: List decisions you feel the team should be making, but isn't yet.

_____

_____

_____

_____

_____

• *Is more information or training needed first?*

_____

_____

_____

_____

Chapter **13**

Managing Conflict

Conflict is often cited as one of the main reasons people dislike working in teams. Since conflict is inevitable, teams need to find a way to manage it

TEAM EXERCISE

Conflict Management

Instructions: INDIVIDUAL TASK - Read each statement once. Indicate whether you (A) agree or (D) disagree with each statement. TEAM TASK - As a team, discuss your individual answers and then reach consensus* on whether you agree or disagree with each statement. (You can change the wording of the statements in order to reach agreement.)

Key: "A" if you agree; "D" if you disagree.

(　　) 1. A Team Member should say everything he/she is thinking and feeling.

(　　) 2. A Team Member should give feedback only when it's asked for.

(　　) 3. Sometimes it's better to just withdraw from the discussion rather than fight.

(　　) 4. A Team Member should stick to his/her opinion of what's right no matter what others do.

(　　) 5. Negotiating agreement is always possible.

(　　) 6. Conflict should never get emotional or personal.

(　　) 7. It is possible for a Team Member to be too agreeable.

(　　) 8. Team cohesiveness is more important than anything else.

(　　) 9. Peer appraisals only lead to conflict.

(　　) 10. When a Team Member is asked to do something he/she doesn't want to do, he/she should do it anyway.

*"Guidelines for Reaching Consensus" on page 37.

Continued on next page

(   ) 11. Conflict can be exciting, creative, and fun.

(   ) 12. A Team Member should never take the side of someone outside the Team over a Team Member.

(   ) 13. It is impossible to have a good relationship with everyone on the Team.

(   ) 14. There is less conflict with people you trust.

(   ) 15. Team Members have less conflict when they do not socialize outside of work.

(   ) 16. A Team Member should always support the consensus decisions made by the Team.

(   ) 17. Understanding is more important than agreement.

(   ) 18. Some members of a Team will just never get along.

(   ) 19. Conflict is totally unproductive.

(   ) 20. Beware of reaching agreement too easily and quickly.

(   ) 21. The Team Leader/Facilitator needs to settle all conflicts.

(   ) 22. The Team needs to develop ground rules for handling conflicts.

Questions:

1. At what points did conflict occur during the consensus exercise you just finished on conflict management?

_____

_____

_____

_____

_____

2. Was the conflict resolved?

_____

_____

(If, yes, how was it resolved?)

_____

_____

_____

_____

_____

3. As you think about it, what issues, problems, etc. usually create conflict within the team?

_____

_____

_____

_____

_____

4. What behaviors (individual & team) escalate the conflict/s?

_____

_____

_____

_____

_____

5. What behaviors (individual & team) help resolve the conflict/s?

_____

_____

_____

_____

_____

When everyone is finished, discuss your answers with the team.

Notes:

INDIVIDUAL EXERCISE

What's Your Conflict Style?

Over time we have all developed different styles for handling conflict. These habits may be helping us or hindering us. It is very important to become aware of our personal style, the consequences of that style, and learn what the alternatives are so we can choose what's most helpful and productive.

Think about 3 recent conflicts you have had at work. Describe what happened, what you did, and what the outcome was:

Conflict 1: The situation?

_____

_____

_____

_____

_____

What *you* did?

_____

_____

_____

_____

_____

The outcome?

_____

_____

_____

_____

_____

Conflict 2: The situation?

_____

_____

_____

_____

_____

What *you* did?

_____

_____

_____

_____

The outcome?

_____

_____

_____

_____

Conflict 3: The situation?

_____

_____

_____

_____

_____

What *you* did?

_____

_____

_____

_____

The outcome?

_____

_____

_____

_____

_____

As you think about all 3 conflicts, what patterns do you see?

_____

_____

_____

_____

_____

Determining Your Conflict Style

Keeping these three incidents you just described in mind, let's try to determine which of the following is your prevalent conflict style.

Style 1: AVOIDANCE

Some people will do anything to avoid conflict. They will agree simply for the sake of harmony and even hold back their own good ideas. Sometimes this is caused by fear of emotional confrontation that stems from myths about human behavior. "It's not nice to fight." "If you don't have something good to say, don't say anything." Acting on these myths, people who avoid conflict are not as productive as they could be. Teams need to create an atmosphere where everyone will express their ideas and opinions without fear of ridicule or criticism. Team members who avoid conflict need to be reassured that their voice counts, they will not be ridiculed, and that disagreement is natural and healthy. One way to draw-out team members that avoid conflict is to make sure *everyone* is heard from before a decision is made. The result will be better solutions to problems (higher quality decisions) and everyone's commitment to carry out the decision.

Style 2: COMBATIVE

This style is the opposite of the first style. Combative people give their opinions, ideas, suggestions, etc. very quickly, often without thinking about the consequences. They are emotional and direct with their words so you always know where they stand, but they are so abrasive that people get offended by what they say and, especially, how they say it. Being combative comes across as mean and uncaring, when, in fact, it may come from very good intentions. However, the consequences of this style for the team is that other team members become fearful of saying anything that might be ridiculed or criticized. As other team members say less, a combative person can dominate the team. After a while, people begin to resist the combative person's ideas, even good ones. Teams need to help combative people become more aware of the consequences of their style. Making sure everyone is heard from before decisions are made is helpful and so is setting a time limit so a speaker has only a certain amount of airtime and no one person dominates. Combative people need help in seeing that their style causes win-lose games to occur and this is the opposite of what they want. They can actually achieve more by choosing their words more carefully, weighing consequences before they blurt things out, and listening more than they talk.

Style 3: COLLABORATIVE

A story frequently told in negotiation seminars tells of two girls fighting over the same orange. Their mother finally intervenes and cuts the orange in half. The first girls throws away the orange peel and eats the fruit. The second girl throws away the fruit and uses the peel to bake a cake. If the two girls had collaborated, they would have seen that underneath their conflict were needs that were not in conflict. In other words, a win-win solution can usually be found. Collaborative people don't assume there has to be a winner and there has to be a loser. Instead, they communicate with the people they're in conflict with and, eventually, come to a mutually agreed on solution that both parties can live with. This style achieves a balance over the other two styles. A collaborative team member does not avoid conflict, but doesn't create it unnecessarily either. Team members must learn to be collaborative and work through conflict to arrive at win-win solutions because win-lose solutions leave hurt feelings which hinder the ability to work together day-after-day.

Action Commitments:

1. In the 3 situations you described, which of the three conflict styles did you use most often? (avoidance? combative? collaborative?)

_____

_____

_____

2. What do you as an individual need to STOP DOING (as it pertains to handling conflict)?

_____

_____

_____

3. What do you need to START DOING?

_____

_____

_____

Teams need to agree on ground rules for managing conflict. Here are some things to keep in mind as you and your team form your ground rules:

■ Conflict is natural and inevitable. When two or more people interact, there is bound to be some conflict.

■ Conflict can be constructive. Too much agreement or "Group Think" can be unproductive. If people are too agreeable, nothing creative may ever occur.

■ Out of conflict can come greater commitment. Beware of reaching agreement too easily and too quickly. It may mean that people are not voicing concerns they have and the final decision does not have the commitment of the entire team.

■ Be aware of when rigid positions are being maintained instead of staying open.

■ Try to help each other see what's best for the team and look beyond self-interest.

■ Keep in mind these common barriers to collaboration:
- poor listening
- wanting to be "right" at all costs
- believing there is only one "best" way (your way)
- placing blame vs. focusing on solving the problem
- attacking people not problems
- stereotyping people
- presuming we already know what others think
- not being open & honest
- letting a few people dominate a meeting

- not sharing the same information with everyone
- letting egos, power, status, etc. get in the way

■ Also, keep in mind the following elements in negotiating agreement:
- share information
- build trust
- listen actively to the "words & the music" (feelings are as real as facts)
- try not to judge, evaluate, or criticize before you understand
- stay open to new ways of doing things
- always look for a way to negotiate a win-win solution where each party gains something
- develop a procedure for handling "deadlocks" (more time, more communication, a third party mediator/arbitrator, etc.)
- clarify the key interests and needs of conflicting people and list alternatives that might address these
- when the team is locked in conflict, brainstorm creative options
- paraphrase what has finally been agreed on to make sure true agreement has been reached and there is commitment to carry out the solution

And, finally, remember that conflict is a necessary stage in the development of any team. People have to have conflict before they can really know each other. Groups have to confront each others' differences before they can become high-performing.

TEAM EXERCISE

Ground Rules for Conflict

• Have everyone on your team write one ground rule for handling conflict that they feel is important.

My Individual Ground Rule is_____

_____

_____

• Ask for a volunteer to act as scribe and list all the ground rules on a flip chart. When all are listed, have the team discuss each one and decide which ones they want to adopt, drop, reword, clarify, etc. Write the final list here:

Our Team's Ground Rules for Managing Conflict:

_____

_____

_____

_____

_____

_____

_____

_____

_____

Chapter 14

Motivation and Rewards
(Intrinsic and Extrinsic)

Using motivation & rewards
to help teams succeed

INDIVIDUAL
EXERCISE

Motivation Assumptions

Step 1: Read through the following statements and put an (A) next to the statements you as an individual agree with. Place a (D) next to the statements you disagree with.

(   )   1.   There are some rewards more important than money.

(   )   2.   People want to be treated as adults.

(   )   3.   Everyone is different and the same (in many ways).

(   )   4.   A "good job" can fulfill a person's basic, social, and higher-level needs.

(   )   5.   Motivation comes from the inside—it is not something you do to people.

(   )   6.   People want to participate in decisions involving them personally.

(   )   7.   People are goal-centered.

(   )   8.   Technical competence and interpersonal competence are both needed by an effective leader.

(   )   9.   A healthy person never stops learning and growing.

(   ) 10.   An effective leader has to be "situational," that is, take into consideration the individual, the task, and the situation.

(   ) 11.   People like working in teams.

(   ) 12.   A growing person is never satisfied completely.

(   ) 13.   Group decisions are better than one individual's decision.

Continued on next page

(   ) 14. A person needs to manage his/her own job: the planning, the doing, the evaluating, and the improving.

(   ) 15. A person's feelings are as real as physical laws and must always be taken into consideration.

(   ) 16. People are capable of solving their problems if they are given information, resources and support.

(   ) 17. Fear is a mover; not a motivator.

(   ) 18. Reward is more effective than punishment.

(   ) 19. People are either motivated or not motivated.

(   ) 20. Self-direction requires a higher level of motivation.

(   ) 21. The unsatisfied needs of a human being motivate that person; a satisfied need is no longer a motivator.

(   ) 22. Work can play a vital role in a person's life, if it is keyed to the needs of the individual.

(   ) 23. Work team members influence each other's motivation.

(   ) 24. The climate of an organization has an effect on a person's motivation.

(   ) 25. Quality customer service can only be achieved with motivated employees.

(   ) 26. Money is a very important motivator.

TEAM EXERCISE

Step 2: When everyone on your team has finished marking each statement, discuss your opinions as a team and attempt to reach consensus* on each statement. (You can change the wording of a statement to achieve consensus.*) (Suggested Time: 30 minutes)

Step 3: When the team is finished, discuss the following questions:

■ Which statements made for the most "interesting" discussion?

■ Did you learn anything about each other? (Example: Team members

*"Guidelines for Reaching Consensus" on page 37.

often learn that they have different definitions for words like: motivation, goal-centered, effective, mover, etc.)

■ How did you resolve conflict?

Step 4: Each of the 26 statements you just reached consensus on are discussed below. See how your answers compare with these.

1. There are many rewards that are more important than money and some cost little or nothing. Recognition, positive feedback, a "pat-on-the-back," a sincere "thank you," praise, etc. In addition, self-directed work team members get more responsibility, job variety, autonomy, decision-making, teamwork, business information, customer information and a sense of growing and developing, which are all very rewarding. Now, we're not saying that money isn't important— it's very important. And organizations that link monetary rewards to performance, achieve a win-win between themselves and their people. (Number 26 will take a closer look at this very important issue.) So, money is very important, but for a long time traditional American management thought money was the only thing people cared about, and when workers expressed dissatisfaction and lacked motivation, we increased their wages. We've found that's not enough. People need interesting work, need to be multi-skilled, need to know how the whole system works and understand their part in it. They need to know the customer's expectations and be supported in doing good work they can be proud of.

2. Most people want to be treated as adults. Exceptions are people that have become very dependent on authority figures telling them what to do. These people will need coaching and support in learning to take responsibility for their work and not depending on others to tell them what to do, when to do it and how to do it.

3. Of course, all human beings are similar in many ways but we are also different. Each of us have different needs based on unique past experiences, different stages of life, different goals for the future. Respecting each other's diversity is very important and the key to that is understanding each other and having empathy for the other person. That's why we've been stressing the importance of really listening because we believe out of that comes respect. If we really get to know someone, we begin to catch a glimpse of what it's like to walk in their shoes. And, it would be such a boring world if we were all alike!

4. Yes, a good job can fulfill a person's basic needs (security, food, shelter, survival) and social needs (respect of peers, a sense of belonging, a sense of achievement) and if we're very lucky, the work itself can also fulfill higher-level needs (to be the best we can be). We would do this work even if we didn't get paid for it because we like it (most of the time). Some people fulfill these higher-level self-actualizing needs off the job in some recreational form and work provides the money for this.

5. In order to determine whether motivation is internal or external, we need to define the term. Here is one definition

of motivation: "The needs or desires one has to enter into activities that lead to certain goals." In other words, motivation begins with our internal needs (basic, social, and self-actualizing). These needs lead us into certain activities or behaviors that hopefully lead to goals that will satisfy those needs. Hunger, for example, is a need that leads to a behavior like hunting or cooking that fulfills a goal (food).

According to psychologist Abraham Maslow, who studied the motivation of healthy people, all human beings have internal needs. These needs form a hierarchy that can be portrayed like this:

Needs Hierarchy

Basic Needs are survival (air, food, water, sex, shelter, sleep) security, and safety. These needs are the most powerful because we would do almost anything to survive.

The next level, **Social Esteem Needs** (love, belonging, esteem of others, sense of accomplishment, achievement, etc.) are also very important.

If we have our basic and social needs pretty-well satisfied, then we can develop our higher level needs for **Self-Actualization.** Self-actualization is our need to be at our best; achieving our full potential. People who love their work are very fortunate because they self-actualize on the job doing the work itself. (Writers, artists, athletes, etc. might be examples of this). Many people self-actualize outside of work. These are the activities that we enjoy so much we even spend money to do them (sports, hobbies, etc.)

Motivation comes from inside us. Everyone is motivated because everyone is fulfilling some need. Human behavior is not random or accidental; it attempts to reach a goal that satisfies a need.

Motivation is not something you do to people; they are already motivated. Our task is to find out what needs a person is trying to fill and help them. If we block people from filling their needs, that may only make the need stronger, it doesn't make the need go away. What we need to do instead is to help people channel their needs into constructive behavior.

Implications of Needs Theory:

■ Motivation is the energy that helps us satisfy our basic, social and higher level needs. We all know what motivation looks like at work: People who are responsible, committed, and striving to do their best. A motivated workforce can accomplish almost anything.

■ When people are clearly not motivated at work, we need to understand what needs are not being met and see what we can do.

■ Self-directed work teams offer the opportunity for increasing motivation by helping people satisfy their basic needs for security by becoming multi-skilled, constantly learning and developing, growing their company, being world-class competitive, and continually improving.

■ If rewards are tied to performance improvements, a person's sense of financial security is also increased.

■ The teamwork provided by SDWTs also satisfies very important social needs.

■ Doing work one can take pride in, might even approach self-actualization.

6. Most people want to participate in decisions that involve them unless they've become very dependent on outside forces making all their decisions and responsibility, therefore, scares them. They will need support in strengthening their self-esteem and training to help them feel confident enough to make good decisions.

7. People are goal-centered in the sense that all their behavior is done to meet some need. We're not talking about only lofty goals here, but very basic ones like the goal of getting up in the morning. Everything we do is done to reach a goal that satisfies a basic, social, or higher level need. Unfortunately, we sometimes enter into behavior that reaches a goal that does not really satisfy a need. Addiction is an example of this type of behavior. The need is self-esteem (to feel good about oneself) and the behavior is use of alcohol or drugs which only makes one feel good temporarily and never really satisfies the need. In fact, each time it takes larger amounts to produce the desired effect and self-esteem decreases.

8. In a perfect world, leaders would have both knowledge of the work (technical competence) and interpersonal competence. Leaders with only interpersonal competence must be very good listeners and rely on others in order to overcome a lack of technical competence. Effective leaders must have interpersonal competence (be a good communicator, listener, motivator, etc.) in order to understand what individuals and teams need and provide those resources.

9. A healthy person never stops learning and growing. When we've satisfied one need, another pops up. We never

run out of needs. If we're not fulfilling our basic needs, we have endless social needs for esteem and achievement. If we are healthy, we never run out of things we want to learn, experience, try, and experiment with. Out of that comes continual growth and development.

10. An effective leader has to be "situational" and take into consideration the individual (we all have different needs), the task, and the situation. Too often, leaders mistakenly assume that everyone has the same needs as they do. The truth is that leaders often have much stronger control and achievement needs, while employees may have stronger social or basic needs. Therefore, leaders need to get to know their people because only then will they be able to understand the needs that motivate them and make sure the tasks and the people are well-suited. By understanding the needs of people, a leader can then choose the leadership style appropriate to the situation. Some people, especially new employees, will need more direction; others will need little or none. Leaders have to choose their style according to what will best fit the situation. Too often, leaders employ only one style—the one they're most comfortable with, and it may not be the best one for the person, the task, or the situation.

11. Most people like working in effective teams. Human beings are social animals and true hermits are rare. Everyone needs training in teamwork and time to learn this new way of working. If, after this, a few people still want no part of SDWTs, they will have to be given choices.

12. A growing person is never satisfied completely. Our unsatisfied needs are the ones that motivate us and we never run out of needs.

13. Group decisions are better than one individual's decision if the decision has quality and commitment. (Chapter 12 presents an in-depth look at decision-making.) A group decision has many advantages over one individual: if provided with the right information, a group can tap everyone's wisdom and expertise, therefore, making a higher quality decision. And chances are they will have more commitment for carrying it out and making it succeed than they would if the decision was made by one person and then imposed. We tend to support that which we are involved in creating.

14. Most employees are capable of, and want to manage the planning, the doing, the evaluating, and the improving of their job. People who do not may lack proper training, may have become passive and dependent, or may be afraid to take responsibility. But most people find autonomy very rewarding in terms of increased self-esteem, achievement, etc. The reason SDWTs are so successful is that they give workers the job of managing their own work, so leaders can do other things: support teams, do long-range planning, etc.

15. A person's feelings are as real as physical laws and must always be taken into consideration. How we feel about someone or something is very important and real. We always need to be aware of and sensitive to our own feelings and the feelings of others and take feelings into account.

16. We need to have the state of mind that believes that people are capable of

solving their problems if they are given information, resources, and support. We have to "teach people to fish" and not always "give them a fish" if we are to develop people and not make them dependent. There will always be rare exceptions, but if we believe that most people can solve problems given the right information, resources, and support, then they probably will. Our beliefs become self-fulfilling prophecies. The Great Depression was a dramatic example of this phenomenon. People made a run on banks because they were afraid they'd lose their money. Ironically, the banks were solvent until everyone withdrew their funds. Negative expectations caused the very thing people did *not* want to happen. Our beliefs/expectations of other people can do the very same thing. We're so afraid Johnny will turn out badly, that we're always telling him he's bad and had better change. As a result he sees himself as bad and acts accordingly. Children know/sense our expectations and base their beliefs about themselves on how others see them. Years ago an experiment was performed where teachers were told that some of the children in their grade school class were "gifted." Actually, these children were average according to tests. After a year of being treated like gifted children by their teachers, the children were retested and all showed much better than average gains on their standardized tests. The teachers believed these children were gifted, treated them accordingly, and the children rose to meet those expectations. Unfortunately, negative expectations also come true. What we need to do then, is to understand our expectations, and change the negative ones before they do us and others damage. In a team it is important to see everyone as a resource, adding value, capable of learning, growing, and improving.

17. Fear is a "mover," not a motivator. Think for a minute about the difference between a scared person and a motivated person. People who are afraid are reduced to the basic need level where they are afraid for their survival or that they're going to lose something. In this frame of mind they are very dependent, not capable of making good decisions, more prone to errors, and unable to take risks. This is not the kind of worker that makes a company world-class competitive. Layoffs are a good illustration of this. People either become so worried about their jobs that they cannot do their best work or they put all their energy into looking for another job.

18. Reward is more effective than punishment in that it says to people, "Do more of this." Punishment merely says no and doesn't indicate what to do. Reward is a more effective way to develop higher levels of performance.

19. We tend to see people as either motivated at work or not motivated when, in fact, all people are motivated. What we call not motivated are people who are not "turned-on" by what they're doing. Organizations who want to succeed in the 90s and beyond will have to have a motivated workforce. SDWTs increase the variety of a person's work. Narrow jobs become whole (well-defined products or services are produced). People learn various skills and do not have to do one dull, monotonous job all day long. Teamwork fills social needs and problem-solving and decision-making add empowerment, responsibility, and accountablilty. All of these elements of SDWTs plus continuous learning provide a more motivating climate than that of traditional organizations.

20. Self-direction requires a higher level of motivation. A SDWT member is constantly learning, adapting to changes, making decisions, gathering information, communicating with peers/ support people/ customers/ vendors/ suppliers. All of this requires highly motivated people, and an organization attuned to: rewarding performance, listening to new ideas, removing barriers, training, growing, and developing their greatest resource—people.

21. Our unsatisfied needs are the ones that motivate us. If I've just eaten, food will not motivate me until later when I get hungry again. Other needs, like esteem, if developed at a very early age, may not need to be constantly satisfied. We're all different, but all of us have unsatisfied needs that drive us to do the things we do. We need to understand our own needs (which change at different stages of our life) and the needs of others because these are the sources of motivation.

22. Work plays a vital role in everyone's life. We spend a good part of our lives at work. For some people work is all there is, for other's it's a means to an end, but for all of us good work makes a difference. What is good work? Work that fulfills our basic needs, social needs, and if we're really fortunate, the work itself is self-actualizing.

23. Work team members influence each other's motivation. Let's look at the factors that a researcher named Frederick Herzberg identified as affecting job attitudes, and see which ones work team members can influence. Herzberg identified 14 factors: achievement, recognition, the work itself, responsibility, advancement, growth, company policy and administration, supervision, work conditions, salary, relationships with peers, personal life, status, and security. It is easy to see that work team members bring influence to bear on all of these. SDWTs give team members an ever-expanding area of influence so that ultimately people feel that they make a difference to each other and to the organization.

24. The climate of an organization has a significant impact on one's motivation. When a person is first hired, they usually have motivation. What happens to them afterwards determines if that motivation increases (with more and more needs being satisfied) or whether their motivation is blocked and decreases. Looking at Herzberg's list again, think of all the **tools an organization has at its disposal to increase motivation:**

- work assignment
- recognition
- achievement
- training
- learning
- promotion
- benefits
- leadership
- safe physical environment
- salary
- relationships
- responsibility
- teamwork
- status
- security

Too often, motivated people become turned off as they feel their good ideas for improvements are not listened to, their creativity is stifled in favor of doing things "the same old way," they are not trained and developed, they don't feel cared for and they don't feel rewarded or recognized.

25. Only motivated employees can routinely deliver exceptional service.

Think for a moment of yourself as a customer. I'll bet that every time you walk into a store you can tell (within minutes) how that employee serving you feels about the organization they're representing. Customers define quality and only employees motivated to listen and empowered to act on what they hear will make their companies world-class competitive.

26. Money is a very important motivator! Most people agree that our present system of paying people doesn't work very well:

> **A survey by the Public Agenda Foundation interviewed 845 blue and white collar workers and found that 45% believed there was no link between their performance and their pay.**

The Importance of Reward Systems:

When organizations are redesigned into self-directed work teams, they can achieve their greatest gains when reward systems are also changed. SDWTs bring variety, challenge, and many other motivators to work, but people working harder/smarter also want to be financially rewarded. It's a genuine win-win when the company and the people share profits/gains.

Companies are beginning to see the wisdom in this. Fortune Magazine ("Here Come Richer, Riskier Pay Plans," Dec. 1988) reported that incentive pay was spreading into manufacturing and service industries of all types.

> **The American Productivity & Quality Center reports 75% of employers in 1988 used at least one form of nontraditional pay.**

All of these plans attempt to link pay with performance. The challenge is to design an effective pay system that really motivates people and rewards them for working harder/smarter and rewards the company by improving the bottom line and forwarding the strategic plan.

According to many experts, most plans don't work because of poor design (quantity rewarded-but quality suffers) or poor administration (employees don't understand how it works and don't see how what they do makes a difference).

Incentive Compensation Systems That Work:

PROFIT-SHARING: This is the most widely used compensation incentive (more than 30% of US companies). Employees receive an annual bonus which varies depending on the company's profits for that time period. It pays only if the company has profits deemed sufficient to pay-out. It is simple to administer and easy to explain and understand. However, annual payments seem too long to adequately motivate and often employees feel that what they do doesn't have as much impact on the profits as key decisions made by other people (top executives, customers, etc.)

GAINSHARING: Many experts think this is the best incentive system for motivating people. If a unit of an organization (plant, division, department, etc.) surpasses a predetermined goal, all members share in a bonus. This rewards employees for results (producing a product, delivering a service, etc.), they can influence, measure, track, and improve. Gainsharing also encourages teamwork, trust, and employee involvement.

LUMP-SUM BONUSES: Employees receive a one time cash payment. This holds down wage and salary increases, thus controlling fixed costs. In order for this to work, employees must trust management or they might feel the payouts are subjective and unfair.

PAY-FOR-SKILLS, PAY-FOR-KNOWLEDGE: Under this plan, an employee's salary or wage increases each time he/she masters a task or skill block. Mastery needs to be defined and then tested. When a company's strategic plan involves people becoming multi-skilled and learning a lot of new jobs, job consolidation, or continuous improvment, this form of incentive can be very effective. In order to make this work required skills need to be identified and assigned a pay grade. Needs assessment and training also play a critical role. When this is done successfully, employees become multi-skilled, the company gains more flexibility, and everyone wins. The training costs are substantial, but the increased skill levels of people, the effectiveness of teams, and the ability of everyone to solve problems increases. As change accelerates and companies need to constantly improve, pay-for-skills/pay-for-knowledge will reward people for constantly learning. Companies that do this will have the competitive edge over those that don't.

What is Needed to Make Incentive Plans Effective:

■ A Clear Business Strategy. Tie incentives to the company goals, more production, higher quality, better customer service, more skills, lower costs, etc.

■ Involve employees in designing a customized system that fits the uniqueness of your organization.

■ Management must be willing to listen, act on ideas, and share information.

■ Focus on what can be measured. Benchmark performance and track results.

■ Separate incentives from base pay to emphasize the link between the employee's performance and rewards.

■ Be flexible and change the system as conditions change (keep making it better and more effective).

■ Make sure employees understand the plan and know what they need to do to make a difference.

■ Some of the most successful plans combine the best features of many different types of reward systems.

Companies Using Incentive Systems

We are seeing an increase in incentive programs with 26% of U.S. companies using some form of gainsharing.

■ **Corning, Inc.** announced this year that eventually all their plants will have a gainsharing program where all employees will benefit from the productivity of their plant.

■ At **Carrier Corp.** employees participate in "Improshare," When workers produce more acceptable quality goods compared to their benchmark, the resulting savings in labor costs are split 50-50 between the company and the employees (everybody from maintenance workers to machinists to managers gets the same percentage bonus). The result has been increased teamwork, 24% higher productivity, and a lower reject rate.

■ At **Lincoln Electric** there is no hourly rate. Workers get a piecework rate and yearly merit ratings based on their dependability, ideas, quality, and output. Based on these ratings, employees receive year-end bonuses that average 97.6% of their regular earnings. Lincoln Electric has had impressive results: 54 years without a losing quarter and 40 years without layoffs.

■ **Nucor Steel's** plan uses profit-sharing on top of small group incentives. Factory workers at 5 steel mills earn weekly bonuses based on the number of tons of acceptable quality steel they produce. Productive teams average well over 100% of their base pay. Base wages are kept low, but total earnings are higher than the industry average. Workers who are late lose their bonus for the day and workers who are more than 30 minutes late lose their bonus for the week. Manager's salaries are also based on plant productivity; they receive bonuses based on return on plant assets. Plant managers receive bonuses based on overall return on equity. At times managers can suffer even though workers continue to earn bonuses based on output. At the end of the year, Nucor distributes 10% of pretax earnings to all employees. The results: In 1987 Nucor turned out more than twice as much steel as its larger competitors. Ken Iverson, the CEO, credits much of this to Nucor's incentive plan which makes each crew want to make more money than the previous shift so production rises all day long. They haven't had a losing quarter since '65 and no layoffs for over 20 years.

TEAM EXERCISE

As a Team discuss and make a list of: The actions we as a Team need to take to help each Team Member's motivation.

_____

_____

_____

_____

_____

_____

_____

_____

Do the same for actions our organization needs to take to increase the motivation of the work force.

_____

_____

_____

_____

_____

_____

_____

_____

Chapter 15

Facilitating the Adult Learner

A summary of what's critical
to adult learning

Facilitating the Adult Learner 15

Working in self-directed teams is a major learning experience for everyone involved. One of the great challenges will be facilitating the learning of other team members as you learn yourself. Some of the new learnings you'll be facilitating will be: the new attitudes and concepts involved with self-direction, team skills, administrative skills, and cross-training each other in technical skills. All of this requires some basic knowledge of Adult Learning Theory.

The following is a summary of what is needed in order for Adult Learning to be successful:

1. Adults learn best in a physically and psychologically comfortable learning climate.

Learning climate is made of the physical surroundings, the people involved, and the intangible elements (trust level relationships, etc.). Climate affects learning either positively or negatively. Adults learn best in a relaxed, comfortable atmosphere where they feel a degree of control, can ask questions, have impact on pace, learn from each other, risk making mistakes, and ask for clarification. Long lectures and a lot of sitting can detract form learning. Participative, involving activities, group work, and practice sessions enhance learning. Learning can even be fun and when people are having fun, they are at their best—creative, able to take risks, etc. And they'll want more of it, if it's fun!

2. Adults must want to learn.

Adults only learn what they want to learn; they can't be ordered, coerced, or threatened into learning. An adult has to be motivated by some internal need to master a new skill or change an attitude. A facilitator needs to help the adult learner get in touch with what his/her developmental needs are and link new learning to these needs.

3. The skills learned must be practical.

Adults want to learn skills they can use and apply. As change accelerates, everyone at work needs to learn new skills to keep up. Pay-for-skills/pay-for-knowledge reward systems help by compensating people for learning new skills they can use right away and in the process, broaden their skill and knowledge base becoming more valuable to the organization and on the job market in general.

4. Adults have a need to be self-directing.

Adults need to have a sense of control and independence in their learning. Self-paced learning, projects, participative learning, etc. all help give adults a sense that they are directly involved in their learning and have control over its pace and direction.

5. Adults must be involved in their learning.

Adults have a need to be involved in diagnosing their needs, formulating learning goals, and evaluating their learning. For all these reasons participative learning methods are most successful with adults. Adults like problem-based learning, experiential (learning-by-doing) designs, group interaction, etc. All these activities foster needs adults have to be independent, in control, and involved.

6. Adults already have a lot of knowledge and experience from which to draw.

Adults need to feel that they are acknowledged as already having a lot of knowledge and life experience. They need to be able to integrate the new learnings with what they already know. Then, the new ideas, skills, attitudes, will be seen as practical and useful.

7. The adult learner's uniqueness must be acknowledged and a variety of learning experiences provided.

All people are different and learn in different ways. Learning design must be varied to accommodate all types of diversity. Some people learn best by reading, others by doing things with their hands, other people are more visual. Good learning designs accommodate all these learning styles by containing a variety of experiences which all reinforce each other. Learners are also at different life stages, have different cultural experiences, and may have different values. All of these things affect learning and need to be understood by the facilitator. Learners also have different expectations and these need to be stated at the very outset of the learning experience so they can be taken into account. If they are unrealistic, that needs to be acknowledged.

8. Adults need a learning design that facilitates mastery.

Mistakes are difficult for adults because their self-esteem suffers. As adults we're supposed to know how to do things (or so we think) and errors hurt our egos even though they are a natural and unavoidable part of learning. A facilitator needs to be sensitive to this and design the learning in steps and at a pace that facilitates mastery.

9. Adults like learning from each other.

Adults like learning in groups and one-on-one. Adults see others as resources, guides, and supporters and can learn a great deal in pairings, triads, and small group exercises.

10. The facilitator needs to be "other-person" centered.

The attitude of the facilitator toward the learner is crucial. The "self-fulfilling prophecy" phenomenon can come true. When we believe people will fail, they often do. And when we believe people are gifted, they will also live up to those expectations. Much of this is because our attitude manifests itself in different behavior towards the learner. In order to have a "positive" effect on learning, facilitators need to:

- believe the person can succeed with proper support
- be an active listener
- be focused on and sensitive to the learner's needs
- let the learner control the pace (as much as possible)

- encourage questions, clarifications, etc.
- allow some frustration rather than constantly supplying answers
- make the learning as active as possible
- encourage independence
- coach and counsel
- ask for feedback
- give feedback
- design a variety of learning experiences
- value diversity and avoid stereotyping
- ask more than tell
- listen more than talk
- set aside ego
- focus on what the person or the team needs at the particular developmental stage
- view learning as a dynamic, continual process
- build fun into learning (as much as possible—it's not all going to be fun)
- have a lot of patience

11. Learning needs to be seen as a life-long, continual process.
Learning needs to be viewed as not just something children do, but as a way to continue growing, and developing throughout one's lifetime. People never need become obsolete if they continue to learn new attitudes, skills, and strive to reach their full potential.

Notes:

Chapter **16**

Managing Change

**Key questions for
helping people change
themselves & their organizations** ▶

The hardest part of creating successful self-directed work teams is having the right "state of mind." The changes we're talking about require learning a different set of attitudes:

"State-of-Mind" Shift for SDWTs

From:	To:
Many Levels	Flat Organization
Autocratic Style	Participative Style
Directive Decision-making (1 person decides)	Consensus Decision-making (The group decides)
Competitive	Cooperative
"Tell me what to do"	How can *we* work smarter?
"It's Only a Job"	"It's My Job"
Skilled in one job	Constantly Learning
Low Risk-taking	Innovation
Reacting to Change	Seizing Opportunities
Stability & Predictability	Constant Change
Management & Union as Adversaries (Win-Lose)	Management & Union as Partners (Win-Win)
Internal Organization Driven	Customer-Driven
Rules Bound & Slow	Flexible & Fast
Doing Things Right	Doing the "Right" Things
"I only work here"	"I am the company"
Power Over Workers (Told what to do)	Empowered Workforce (Able to do what is right)
"If it's not broken, don't fix it"	Constant Improvement
Acceptable Quality & Service	World-Class Quality & Service
Technology First	People First
People as Spare Parts	People As Valuable Resources
Control of Supervisor	Commitment of Teams
Procedures Book	Self-Control

In order to achieve this state-of-mind we need to believe that the way we've done business for 200 years hasn't ever worked very well, and now it won't work at all.

For 200 years we thought "bigness" was good, so we kept adding layers of people to tell other people what to do, and how to do it. We hired people for narrow jobs, maybe even doing one dull thing all day long, and we hired other people to inspect for quality. We ignored the customer (internal and external).

Despite how poorly this worked, American industry was able to survive because after World War II we had no real competition worldwide and all our competitors within America were also organized this way.

But now things have changed. The successful competitor—and they may be anywhere in the world—is organized very differently.

The Shape of the Successful Organization

1. **FLAT**—As few layers as possible between the work teams (who do the work, plan it, schedule it, build-in quality, make decisions, etc.) and top management.

2. **INFORMATION** is provided directly to the teams so they can make good day-to-day decisions and management can focus on removing barriers, supporting teams, listening to customers and making long-range plans.

3. **FAST**—Decisions are made quickly by multi-skilled, flexible SDWTs who can customize high-quality products at the lowest possible cost.

4. **CONTINUOUS IMPROVEMENT**– Everyone is constantly working on improving something every day, so change is constant.

5. **CUSTOMER-DRIVEN**—Everyone is listening to customers (in a variety of ways: face-to-face, telephone, written feedback, etc.) and acting on what they hear.

6. **QUALITY**—is defined by the customer and it's everyone's responsibility.

7. **CONSTANT TRAINING & LEARNING**—Everyone is constantly learning and training. People are seen as the most valuable resource the company has and an appreciating asset.

8. **SDWTs ARE A PROCESS** - a permanent change in state of mind, culture and way of doing business—not a "program" that has a beginning and an ending. Everyone's job will change as the organization evolves.

9. **PARTNERSHIPS** with unions, vendors, customers who are involved in key decisions.

10. **REWARDS TIED TO MEASUREABLE PERFORMANCE.** Everyone shares in the profits/gains. Every job adds value. Everyone is measured and everyone knows how what they do has impact.

Coping With All This Change

The changes we've been describing are dramatic and we as human beings do not always like change. We cling to our habits even when we know we shouldn't. We dislike change for other reasons also: it's more work (at first), we're afraid of making mistakes (or failing altogether), we'll need to learn new skills, we don't like uncertainty, and we need time to adjust. **The research on change says we go through 4 predictable stages:**

Human beings need time to move through the 4 Stages of Change; it doesn't happen all at once.

We can help people change by:
- ■ Providing Information On:
  - Vision
  - Mission
  - Goals
  - State of Business
  - Support/Training Available
  - Important Questions (i.e., "Why are we doing this?" "What's in it for me?"
- ■ Listening (to words & feelings)
- ■ Not Judging
- ■ Giving Positive Reinforcement
- ■ Role-Modeling New Behaviors
- ■ Coaching/Couseling
- ■ Being Patient

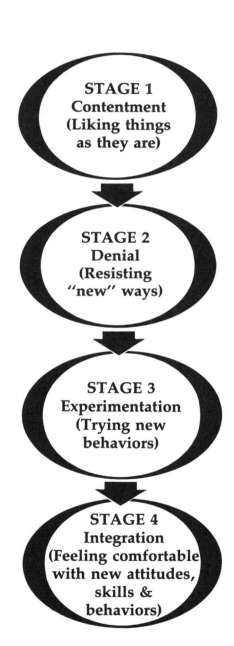

Overcoming Barriers to SDWTs: Our Experience

We have worked with hundreds of people at various stages of changing themselves and their workplaces. We have a set of beliefs on change based on our experience:

■ The key to successful change efforts is employee involvement. People tend to support change when they have played a part in shaping it. If changes are imposed on people, they resist.

■ The vast majority of people are successful in adapting to these new workplaces. Many people (especially front-line workers) feel SDWTs make sense and welcome the changes they bring about.

■ A few people will probably be unwilling to change and they must also be given choices. Usually they can be technical experts supporting teams, or individual contributors.

■ The higher up in the organization one goes; the more difficult it is to understand this new state of mind. This might be true for several reasons. Executives, managers and supervisors tend to see more loss in this than gain (at least at first). Traditional perks are removed, power shifts and roles drastically change. Eventually, there is a sense of gain, but this takes time and patience. All the training and learning that takes place slows things down at first and doesn't pay off for quite some time. When it does, leaders find that they are now free to do many things they always wanted to do to make the organization more effective.

■ Since there are now fewer layers, alternate career paths need to be created so everyone gets a sense of growth without necessarily being promoted to another level. And since there will be fewer supervisors and managers, people need to be rewarded without going into management, so redesigning reward systems becomes important.

■ Everyone needs assurances that productivity gains will not cost them their jobs. Unless this is stated, people will drag their feet and even hold back ideas that put them at risk. It's a lose-lose for the organization and the person.

■ SDWTs could be a permanent change in the way America works or it could be a "program-of-the-month." If it is a program, it will not succeed. It must be seen as a continual, permanent process change in the way we do business.

Questions:

At each stage of change, certain questions need to be answered, again-and-again, to reinforce new behaviors. Some of these important questions for you and your team are: (Answer these as an individual and then discuss them with your team.)

1. Why are we doing this? What is the compelling, driving reason for all this change?

_____

_____

_____

_____

2. Is it important that we do this? What might happen if we don't?

_____

_____

_____

_____

3. Is this change to SDWTs doable?

_____

_____

_____

_____

4. What am I supposed to do?

_____

_____

_____

_____

5. What are my goals, objectives, etc.?

_____

_____

_____

_____

6. How will the organization benefit?

_____

_____

_____

_____

7. How will I benefit?

_____

_____

_____

_____

8. How will this team benefit?

_____

_____

_____

_____

9. How am I doing? (Is there feedback provided to me on how well I'm doing or what mistakes I'm making?)

_____

_____

_____

_____

• *Do the same for how are "we" (the team) doing?*

_____

_____

_____

_____

10. Is support available?

_____

_____

_____

_____

11. Have I received enough training?

_____

_____

_____

_____

• *Has the team received enough training? (Technical? Interpersonal? Administrative?)*

_____

_____

_____

_____

12. What do I see as the "barriers" to this change being successful?

_____

_____

_____

_____

13. What needs to be done to overcome these barriers?

_____

_____

_____

_____

_____

14. What happens if I make a mistake?

_____

_____

_____

_____

15. What are we going to be like when the change has taken place? (Is the vision/mission clear to people?)

_____

_____

_____

_____

16. Other concerns I have:

_____

_____

_____

_____

• Other concerns the Team has:

_____

_____

_____

_____

Chapter 17

Quality Customer Service

**Exercises & questions
for improving
customer service** ▶

The main reason for all this dramatic change we've been talking about is to improve something for our customers.

Research on Quality Customer Service Reveals:

■ The customer defines what quality is and the target is always moving.

■ Everyone has a customer—either an internal customer (people within your company that depend on your work) or an external customer.

■ Satisfying customers is the reason we are in business and satisfying customers is the only guarantee of staying in business.

■ Find out what your customers want. Don't assume you know:
• What your customers want
• How you're doing in serving them
• How you could do better (ask for suggestions)
• What else your customers would like (new products/services)

■ Gather customer information in a number of different ways:
• Face-to-face
• Phone calls (800 numbers)
• Surveys

■ Measure & track your results as a way to improve:
• Quality
• Response time

■ Don't assume because you don't hear complaints that customers are satisfied. According to research:
• 1/3 of customers with problems don't complain; they just *stop* using your services
• An unhappy customer tells 10-15 other people
• Resolve a problem and you will actually build more loyalty to your company than you had before (treat complaints/problems as opportunities)

■ Treat your internal customers as well as your external customers.

■ To the customer, you are the company, therefore, everyone needs to have:
• Telephone Skills
• Listening Skills
• Brainstorming/Problem-Solving sessions that focus on improving Customer Service

Questions:

1. Who is your customer (internal or external or both?)

_____

_____

_____

_____

2. How does your customer define quality?

_____

_____

_____

_____

• How do you know this?

_____

_____

_____

• If you don't know, how could you find out?

_____

_____

_____

TEAM EXERCISE

Improving Customer Service

What does your entire service cycle look like? Diagram it now—Start with: Customer's initial contact

_____

Step #1_____

Step #2_____

Step #3_____

Step #4_____

Step #5_____

Step #6_____

Step #7_____

Step #8_____

Step #9_____

Step #10_____

End with: Service Complete

1. Does everyone on the team have the same understanding of the service cycle? If there are differences, discuss them until you agree.

_____

_____

_____

_____

• What problems (quality, speed, etc.) are there with the cycle—from your point of view?

_____

_____

_____

_____

• From your customer's point of view?

_____

_____

_____

_____

• What could be improved? Eliminated? Shortened? Wasted steps? Redundant paperwork? No value-added steps? Opportunities for redesign? Where do variances (problems) occur? Why?

_____

_____

_____

_____

2. Do your organization's systems, policies, procedures meet the customer's needs or are they strictly for the company's convenience?

_____

_____

_____

_____

3. Do you regularly solicit feedback from your customers in a variety of ways?

_____

_____

_____

_____

4. Do you act on customer feedback? (Name some specific service improvements you've implemented.)

_____

_____

_____

_____

5. Has your team received customer service training lately?

_____

_____

_____

_____

6. How do you handle customer complaints, problems, suggestions?

_____

_____

_____

_____

7. What is your team's stated mission on customer service?

_____

_____

_____

8. List some changes you could make that would delight your customers.

_____

_____

_____

_____

9. Are there obstacles/barriers in your organization to providing quality customer service?

_____

_____

_____

_____

10. Is quality customer service rewarded in your organization?

_____

_____

_____

_____

11. Who is your competition? (Another company? Other sites? Outsourcing? Contract Services?)

_____

_____

_____

12. Any other important considerations your team should address on the subject of customer service?

_____

_____

_____

_____

Action Commitments:

After everyone has shared/discussed their answers, what action commitments does the team want to make at this time to improve customer service?

_____

_____

_____

_____

_____

_____

_____

_____

_____

_____

_____

_____

_____

_____

_____

_____

_____

_____

_____

Chapter 18

Problem-Solving for Continuous Improvement

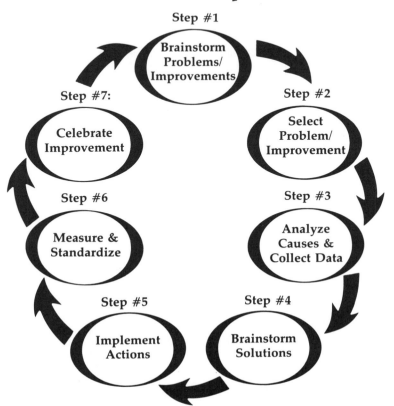

Step #1
Brainstorm Problems/ Improvements

Step #2
Select Problem/ Improvement

Step #3
Analyze Causes & Collect Data

Step #4
Brainstorm Solutions

Step #5
Implement Actions

Step #6
Measure & Standardize

Step #7:
Celebrate Improvement

Defining Continuous Improvement

Continuous Improvement means everyone working, everyday, on improving something. It is an attitude and a philosophy that says, the "same old way" isn't good enough. Everyone needs to work on improving QUALITY, TIMELINESS, SAFETY, etc. by eliminating waste, rework, non-value-added time, unnecessary paperwork, bureaucratic rules and procedures, interruptions, etc.

It is a never-ending journey because there is no limit to the potential of a team of people working constantly on improving things.

As you and your team begin the process of examining what you want to improve, think about the "Big Picture":

Examining How You Do Things Now

Always start with "the customer." A customer can mean internal employees (the people who receive the team's output) and, ultimately, an external customer. To answer the following questions, take into account that the opinion of the internal customer and the external customer are both important. Your team's output may be satisfactory to the internal customer, but when the external customer receives the final product/service, he/she may not be satisfied.

The following questions will help you and your team determine what problems/improvements you need to examine.

Questions:

1. Who is your internal customer?

_____

• External customers?

_____

_____

2. What does your <u>internal</u> customer think about your current level of performance? Rate this as your customers would:

Customer's Name:	Check (✔) One		
	Unsatisfactory	Satisfactory	World-Class
Quality			
Speed			
Service			
Accuracy			
Other things your customers care about:			

• *What do your <u>external</u> customers think about your current level of performance? Rate this as your customers would:*

Customer's Name:	Check (✔) One		
	Unsatisfactory	**Satisfactory**	**World-Class**
Quality			
Speed			
Service			
Accuracy			
Other things your customers care about:			

3. *How do you currently gather feedback from your customers? (questionnaires, 800 numbers, face-to-face dialogs, etc.)*

_____

_____

_____

_____

4. *What are your customer's specific expectations regarding your output?*

_____

_____

_____

_____

5. How does the team currently **measure** *these aspects?*

_____

_____

_____

_____

6. What is your team's current level of performance (the team's opinion)?

_____

_____

_____

_____

7. What level of performance do other organization's achieve?
What are the "world-class" benchmarks the team needs to aim for?

_____

_____

_____

_____

8. Who are your suppliers, what input do they provide you with and what is their current level of performance?

Check (✔) One

SUPPLIERS	INPUT	PERFORMANCE LEVEL		
Name:	Item(s) Supplied	Unsat.	Sat.	World-Class

9. **What areas do your suppliers need to improve?**

_____

_____

_____

_____

10. **How could the team work with suppliers to improve their input?**

_____

_____

_____

_____

_____

11. **What relationships could be improved with:**

Suppliers? _____

_____

_____

Vendors? _____

_____

_____

Support Groups? _____

_____

_____

_____

12. What could be improved in your team's work processes?

_____

_____

Waste? _____

_____

Bottlenecks? _____

_____

Unnecessary Steps? _____

_____

Interruptions? _____

_____

Delays? _____

_____

Layout of Equipment? _____

_____

Variances? (Problems) _____

_____

Tasks simplified or eliminated? _____

_____

Scrap? _____

_____

Safety? _____

_____

Service? _____

_____

Feedback? _____

_____

Information? _____

_____

Other? _____

———————————————————— ★ ————————————————————

_____

7 Step Problem-Solving for Continuous Improvement

TEAM EXERCISE

Step #1: Brainstorm* - Problems/Improvements

List all suggestions for problems/improvements to work on called out by Team Members:

_____

_____

_____

_____

_____

_____

_____

_____

_____

*"Guidelines for Brainstorming" on page 32.

Step #2: Select Problem/Improvement

Have the team vote (by show of hands) which problems/improvements they feel are:

- the most important at this time

- ones the team can implement

- ones that will need outside assistance

- ones that are linked to key customer-based measures

■ After this vote, discuss why people voted as they did. Focus on sharing information so everyone has the same facts to deal with.

■ Then, take another vote to select the *one* item to focus on at this time.

■ Once the team has made their selection, clearly define what the problem/improvement is so everyone shares the same understanding.

The problem/improvement our team has selected to work on at this time is:

_____

_____

_____

_____

_____

_____

Step #3: Analyze Causes

Once your problem/improvement selection has been made, begin to analyze the causes. Begin with a flow chart of the process. What steps are involved in the process from start (input) to finish (output) if the process worked as it should? After reading the example, fill in your "Process Flow Chart" on next page.

Example:
Process Flow Chart For Filling A Book Order

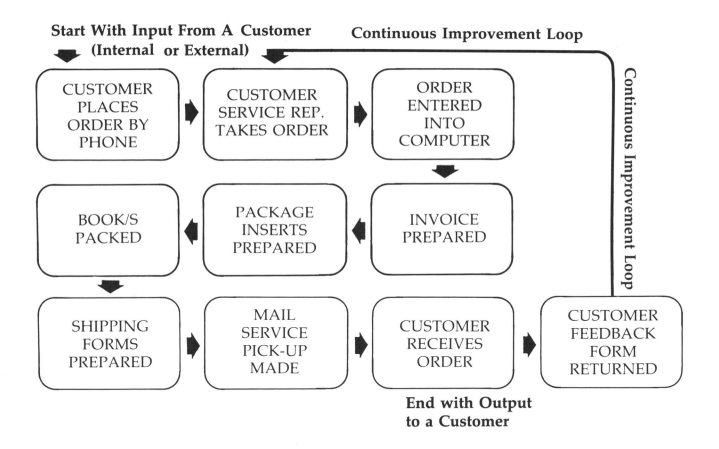

Start With Input From A Customer (Internal or External)

Continuous Improvement Loop

Continuous Improvement Loop

| CUSTOMER PLACES ORDER BY PHONE | CUSTOMER SERVICE REP. TAKES ORDER | ORDER ENTERED INTO COMPUTER |

| BOOK/S PACKED | PACKAGE INSERTS PREPARED | INVOICE PREPARED |

| SHIPPING FORMS PREPARED | MAIL SERVICE PICK-UP MADE | CUSTOMER RECEIVES ORDER | CUSTOMER FEEDBACK FORM RETURNED |

End with Output to a Customer

(Arrows indicate relationship between steps.)

Process Flow Chart

For _____

Name of Process

Start

End

(Indicate with arrows the relationship between the steps).

After the team reaches agreement on the "Process Flow Chart," answer the following questions:

1. Where do the problems, errors (variances) occur?

_____

_____

_____

_____

2. Where do delays (non-value-added time) occur?

_____

_____

_____

_____

3. Is there obvious evidence of redundancy, rework, waste, etc.?

_____

_____

_____

_____

4. What does the team do to obtain feedback from customers?

_____

_____

_____

_____

Step #3: Collect Data

• **WHAT** data is needed?

_____

_____

_____

_____

• **HOW** will we collect this data?

_____

_____

_____

_____

• **WHO** will collect it?

_____

_____

_____

_____

• **WHEN** will it be collected?

_____

_____

_____

_____

As data is collected, it will need to be sorted and there are a variety of methods for doing this. Following are Process Improvement Tools which are all valuable depending on what you're trying to analyze:

Tool #1: Cause & Effect Diagram

A Cause & Effect Diagram (also known as a fish-bone diagram) helps analyze the relationship between some "effect" and all the possible "causes" that might have produced it. As a team, call out all the possible causes of the problem you've selected to analyze. These might be grouped under major headings like, people, equipment, materials, and procedures/policies. Place your answers in the blank diagram on the next page.

Example: Cause and Effect Diagram: Orders Not Delivered on Time

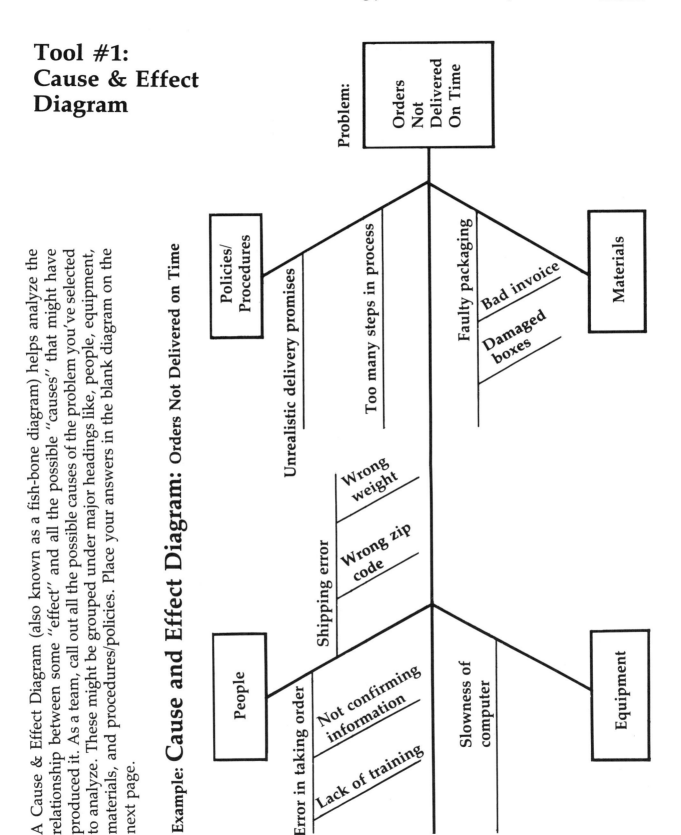

*Instructions: Complete the Cause and Effect Diagram on the next page.

Cause and Effect Diagram

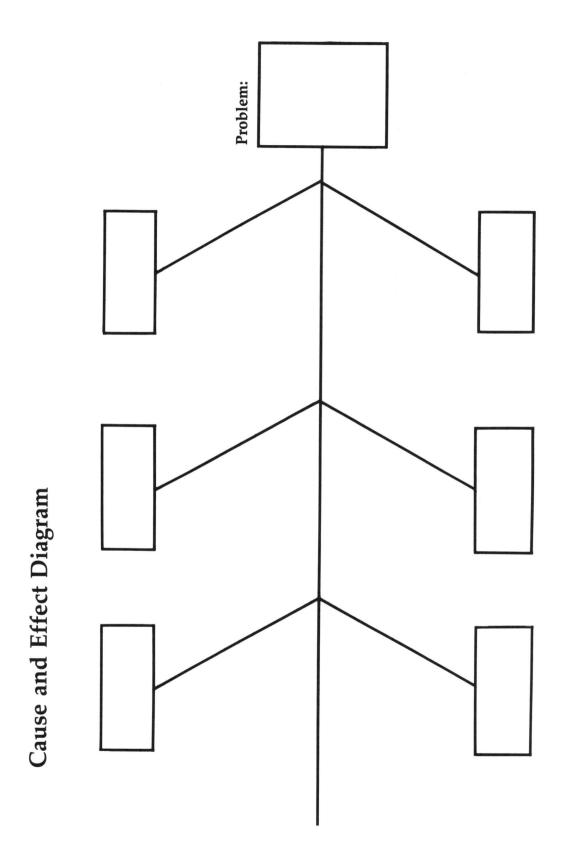

Problem:

Tool #2: Problem Observation Worksheet

A Problem Observation Worksheet is useful for collecting information used on observations.

Problem Being Observed: _____

What is happening?

Where does it happen?

When does it happen?

How often?

When doesn't it occur?

Any other observations or relevant information?

_____

_____

_____

_____

Tool #3:   Check Sheet

A Check Sheet is useful for gathering data in order to begin to see patterns (the frequency of a problem, distribution of occurrence, outcome over a period of time, etc.)

Example:

Copier Problems	Week 1	Week 2	Week 3	Week 4
Paper Jams	//	//	////	⊦⊦⊦ /
Parts Needing Replacement	/	0	//	/
Service Calls	//	//	////	⊦⊦⊦
Total:	5	4	10	12

★

Create your own Check Sheet by:
- Agreeing on the problem/s your measuring.
- Deciding the time frame (hours, weeks, months, etc.)
- Designing a clear, easy, form.

Problem:	Time Frame:
Total:	

Tool #4:   Pareto Chart

A Pareto Chart is a vertical bar graph that enables one to see which problems occur with the most frequency:

Example: Customer Complaints

Number of Times Problem Occurs

```
50
45
40
35
30
25
20
15
10
 5
 0
```

Invoicing | Shipping | Delivery | Packaging | Ordering   **Types of Problems**

★

Problem Selected: _____

FREQUENCY

**VARIABLES FROM
HIGHEST TO LOWEST**

Tool #5:   Scattergram Chart

A Scattergram Chart is useful for showing the relationship between one variable and and another variable.

Example: Relationship Between Billing Errors and Time of Day

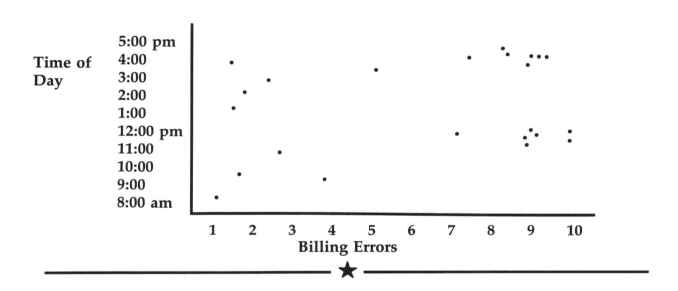

⭐

Relationship Selected _____

VARIABLE 1

VARIABLE 2

Step #4: Brainstorm Solutions

Once enough data is collected and analyzed, the team is ready to brainstorm* solutions. List them here.

Possible Solutions:

_____

_____

_____

_____

_____

_____

_____

_____

_____

_____

_____

_____

_____

_____

_____

_____

_____

_____

*"Guidelines for Brainstorming" on page 32.

Rank Solutions and Make Selections

After list has been completed, vote (by show of hands) on which solutions you want to implement at this time.

- Solutions the Team can implement right now?

- Which ones can only be implemented with added resources (money, time, equipment, etc.)?

- Which ones will have the most impact—short term?   —long term?

Solution/s to Implement

_____

_____

_____

_____

_____

_____

_____

_____

Step #5: Implement Actions

After the Team has selected the solutions to implement, an Action Plan is needed to decide "who" is going to do "what" by "when."

Action Plan			
Meeting Date:			
Problem	**Action**	**Target Date**	**Person/s Responsible**

> **After you've developed an action plan, make sure you communicate it to *all* the people that are going to be involved in doing it or supporting it.**

■ Whose support is the Team going to need?

_____

_____

■ What needs to be done to gain that support needed?

_____

_____

_____

Step #6: Measure & Standardize

1. How is the Team going to measure the results of the action/s taken?

_____

_____

_____

2. What would "good" results look like?

_____

_____

_____

3. If good results are achieved, what needs to be done to make them standard practice by everyone?

_____

_____

_____

Step #7: Celebrate Improvement!

(Make sure suggestions, ideas, and actions are recognized, rewarded, and celebrated.)
This is what our organization does to:

Recognize People & Teams _____

_____

Reward Individuals & Teams _____

_____

Celebrate _____

_____

> Since improvement is a "continual process," select another problem/improvement to work on next.

Chapter 19

For Further Reading

**A Bibliography on
Self-Directed Teams**

Goodman, Paul S. *Designing Effective Workgroups.*
   San Francisco: Jossey-Bass, 1986.

Hackman, J. R. and G. R. Oldham *Work Redesign.*
   Reading, MA: Addisson-Wesley, 1980.

Harper, Ann & Bob. *Self-Directed Work Teams & Your Organization:*
   Two Assessment Tools.   New York: MW Corporation, 1991.

Harper, Ann & Bob. *Succeeding As A Self-Directed Work Team:*
   20 Important Questions Answered.
   New York: MW Corporation, 1990.

Lawler, E. E. *High Involvement Management.*
   San Francisco: Jossey-Bass, Inc., 1986.

Lawler, E. E. *Strategic Pay: Aligning Organizational Strategies and Pay Systems.*
   San Francisco: Jossey-Bass, Inc., 1990.

Likert, Rensis. *New Patterns of Management.*
   New York: McGraw-Hill, 1961.

Nora, John J., C. Raymond Rogers & Robert J. Stamy.
   Transforming the Workplace.   New Jersey: Princeton Research Press, 1986.

Pasmore, William A. *Designing Effective Organizations:*
   The Sociotechnical Systems Perspective.
   New York: John Wiley & Sons, Inc., 1988.

Peters, Tom. *Thriving on Chaos: Handbook for a Management Revolution.*
   New York: Alfred A. Knopf, 1987.

Schonberger, Richard J. *World Class Manufacturing Casebook:*
   Implementing JIT and TQC.
   New York: The Free Press, 1987.

Waterman, Robert H. *The Renewal Factor.*
   New York: Bantam Books, 1988.

Wellins, R. S. *Self-Directed Teams: A Study of Current Practice.*
   DDI, AQP & Industry Week, 1991.

Weisbord, Marvin R. *Productive Workplaces: Organizing & Managing*
   for Dignity, Meaning & Community.
   San Francisco: Jossey-Bass, 1987.

Chapter 20

Products & Services to Support SDWTs

Books, Videos, Tools, Workshops (Public & On-Site)

MW Corporation is a full-service consulting firm offering the following products and services to support your employee involvement and SDWT efforts:

CONSULTING SERVICES

PUBLIC WORKSHOPS:
(Throughout the U.S.)

Self-Directed Work Teams Workshop
The "1990s Manager" Workshop
Supv./Team Leader/Tech. Leader Workshop
Facilitator Workshop
Team Leadership Workshop
Train-the-Trainer Workshop
Active Listening Workshop
Quality Customer Service Workshop
Quality and Continuous Improvement
   Workshop

ON-SITE TRAINING
(Custom-designed)

On all of the above topics plus:
Team Development
Employee Involvement Team Development

Written by **Ann & Bob Harper,** authors of *Succeeding As A Self-Directed Work Team* and *Skill-Building for S-D Team Members*, and filled with high-involvement exercises, checklists and assessments, for participative learning.

ITEM #500

Quantity	Per Copy
1	$34.95
2-24	$24.00
25-99	$22.00
100-299	$20.00
300-599	$17.00
600 +	$15.00

Prices subject to change.

A New Book/Workbook
TEAM BARRIERS:

Actions for Overcoming the: Blocks to Empowerment, Involvement, & High-Performance

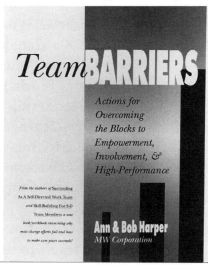

*Team*BARRIERS

Actions for Overcoming the Blocks to Empowerment, Involvement, & High-Performance

From the authors of Succeeding As A Self-Directed Work Team and Skill-Building For S-D Team Members a new book/workbook examining why most change efforts fail and how to make sure yours succeeds!

Ann & Bob Harper
MW Corporation

246 Pages

Learn why MOST change efforts fail & how to make sure yours succeeds!

Examine the BARRIERS that slow teams down or stop their progress altogether. Learn how to overcome the blocks and develop successful High-performing teams.

A must read book for team leaders, team members, HRD, trainers, OD, consultants, educators, etc. Any organization that has or plans to redesign, reengineer, or form teams-needs to read this book.

Table of Contents: (A Partial Description)

Action One: EMPOWERING EVERYONE
- How Empowered Are You? How Empowered Is Your Team?
- A Definition
- Barriers to Empowerment
- Types of Employee Involvement & Degrees of Empowerment
- Barriers to Bldg. High-Performing Teams

Action Two: CHANGING THE "TOTAL" CULTURE
- Why We Have To Change from Traditional to High-Performance • Dealing with Resistance to Change • Questions People Need Answered During Times of Change • Overcoming Barriers to Change • Stages of Change

Action Three: LEADERSHIP THAT "WALKS-THE-TALK"
- Reasons Top Leadership Resists Leading Change Efforts
- Top Leadership's New Role • High-Involvement Exercise • Exerting Influence • Site Visit Questionnaire

Action Four: CREATING A ROADMAP FOR THE TRANSITION
- A 5-Phase Change Model

Action Five: INVOLVING ALL KEY STAKEHOLDERS
- Ten Common Mistakes • Organization Climate Assessment • Critical Questions • Consensus-Building Exercise: the "Essential Ingredients of High-Performance"

Action Six: SHARING DECISION-MAKING POWER
- Criteria for a "Good" Decision • Decisions High-Performing Teams Make • Creating a Transition Plan • High-Involvement Exercise

Action Seven: BUILDING WORK GROUPS INTO "TEAMS"
- Key Elements of High-Performing Teams • Stages of Team Development: Leadership & Training Needed at Each Stage • Continual Learning • Team Effectiveness Assessment

Action Eight: CREATING NEW ROLES FOR LEADERS
- Choosing the Best Leadership Model for Your Organization • The "New Role of the Supervisor" • Why Supervisors & Managers Resist Change • Actions for Building Commitment • "My Leadership Style": Assessment

Action Nine: TRAINING! TRAINING! TRAINING!
- Towards a Learning Organization
- 3 Types of Training Teams Need
- 7 Training Activities: Team Ground Rules; Team Meetings; Communication; Coaching; etc.

Action Ten: CHANGING ORGANIZATIONAL SYSTEMS
- Measurement • Appraisal
- Career Development • Reward

Action Eleven: BUILDING-IN CONTINUOUS LEARNING
- Process Vs. Program • 2 Case Studies

Call 914-528-0888 To Order
(Ask About Quantity Discounts) We Ship Same Day!

"...*the best* quick introduction to self-directed teams..."

Book/Workbook on SDWTs:

Succeeding as a Self-Directed Work Team:
20 Important Questions Answered

For: CEOs, Managers, Team Leaders, Steering Comm./Design Team Members, and Work Team Members

A Quick, Easy to Read, Very User-Friendly Guide to the Most Important Work Innovation to Come Along in the Past 200 Years!

If you don't already have them—you'll want to know how they're revolutionizing the workplace. And why they're producing unbelievable results in quality and productivity in companies that use them.

If you already have SDWTs, you'll want to learn how to maximize the results and make sure yours succeed.

You'll want to read this before your competition does! You'll want all the people in your workforce to read it!

Just Some of the Questions Addressed:

- What are the benefits for the organization?
- What is the new role of Supervisor and Manager?
- What are the benefits for the individual?
- Why work teams now?
- Do they work? What's the evidence?
- What are the possible drawbacks?
- What stages does a SDWT go through and what is needed at each stage?

Quantity	Per Copy
1	$14.95
2-24	$12.00
25-99	$10.50
100-299	$9.00
300-599	$8.00
600 +	$7.50

Plus shipping & handling.

WHAT PEOPLE ARE SAYING ABOUT SUCCEEDING AS A SELF-DIRECTED WORK TEAM:

"...*it's a **must read** for all members of any organization that is considering a culture change toward participatory management. My one regret is that we didn't have it in our possession when we started the process. It would have been the **perfect** 'handbook' for all our people. Congratulations on creating **a valuable tool** for the **teams of the 90s.** "*
Manager
G.E. National Customer Service Center

"*A good, **easy-reading** book that presents **all the key points quickly**. The whole team read it, answered the questions, and discussed them together.*"
Team Member
Traditional Org. Changing
to Self-Directed Work Teams

"*After reading this book, I can see how Self-Directed Work Teams could really work.*"
Union Leader
Manufacturing Plant

"***Best book** I've read on the subject of Self-Directed Teams and why they work. Helped me explain to people what we're trying to do here.*"
Manager of Training and Development

"***A great book.** I'm going to buy one for everyone on the **Steering Committee,** the **Design Teams, Team Leaders,** and eventually the **Team Members** .*"
EI Coordinator

"*Just the book I've been looking for for all our **Facilitators** .*"
Manager Quality Programs

Call 914-528-0888 To Order
(Ask About Quantity Discounts) We Ship Same Day!

New! VIDEOS ON SELF-DIRECTED WORK TEAMS

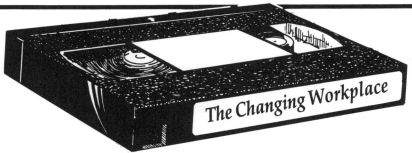

The Changing Workplace

ORDER #V-1 **A TEAM LEADER'S DAY** - Spend a day with a Team Leader managing the boundaries of the Self-Directed Team, encouraging team members to make their own decisions, etc. Listen as she overcomes her anxieties about losing her traditional supervisory role and discovers new satisfactions, responsibilities and success as a facilitator of a High Performance Team. Time: 32 minutes
3-Day Preview $45.00 **Purchase Price $495.00**

ORDER #V-2 **SUPERVISORS** - This video helps Supervisors change their role from traditional supervision to participative team leadership. It presents tough issues in a way Supervisors can recognize and helps them seek their own solution. An empowering experience.
Time: 28 minutes
3-Day Preview $45.00 **Purchase Price $495.00**

ORDER #V-3 **THE CHANGING WORKPLACE** - Ten Managers, Workers, and Supervisors tell how their lives have changed in companies focusing on teamwork, quality and learning. Stimulates important dialogue. Time: 32 minutes
3-Day Preview $45.00 **Purchase Price $495.00**

ORDER #V-7 **IMPROVING WORK SYSTEMS** - Managers, Supervisors, Consultants, and Employees at IDS Financial Services, a division of American Express, recount their experiences in redesigning work. Provides a step-by-step overview of the redesign process. You'll see and hear managers and members talk about how they redesigned a traditional service organization into successful self-managing teams. Time: 27 minutes
1-Week Preview $45.00 **Purchase Price $495.00**

ORDER #V-9 **TOPEKA PRIDE** - See the results of 20 Years of self-directed teams. Learn from one of the most successful applications of self-directed teams. Opened as a "greenfield" production facility in 1971, the Topeka Pet Food factory is America's longest running team-centered work environment. SDWTs on the production floor and in the office manage the day-to-day operations. All Team Members rotate jobs and learn all the skills needed to run this facility as Team Leaders redefine traditional roles. Available in Spanish. Time: 32 minutes
1-Week Preview $45.00 **Purchase Price $495.00**

ORDER #V-8 **LEADING A *SERVICE* TEAM: A DAY WITH A HIGH PERFORMANCE WORK TEAM FACILITATOR** - Spend a day with a Team Facilitator at a financial services company as she gives up control of telephone scheduling, confers with the team about a new quality process, examines her own confidence in the process, encourages initiatives, and deals with the inevitable challenges that arise. Watch as she steps out of the way, supports other team members' efforts, and is excited about the high performance results. Finally, a video about SDWTs in the service sector! Time: 32 minutes
3-Day Preview $45.00 **Purchase Price $495.00**

NEW! JUST RELEASED!

ORDER #V-6 **EVERYBODY LEADS** - In this 26 minute video, you spend a day with the KV-3 team at the Rohm & Haas plant in Lousville, KY. Every team member takes on supervisory tasks like planning, controlling, scheduling, and leading, as well as doing the day-to-day work. The team leader role passes from one worker to another and from shift-to-shift. You get an inside view of how self-managing team members use their leadership skills and process knowledge to make good decisions, handle emergencies, respond to technical problems, increase production, and improve quality.
3-Day Preview $45.00 **Purchase Price $495.00**

ORDER #V-2000 **SELF-DIRECTED WORK TEAMS: REDESIGNING THE WORKPLACE FOR THE 21st CENTURY** - A "nuts-and-bolts" description of what SDWTs are, how they're different from traditional work, why they make for competitive advantage, how leadership is handled by teams, what the "star" model is, how teams schedule work, plan, problem-solve, etc. This video helps people see what SDWTs can do to improve quality, productivity, motivation, etc.
Time: 29 minutes
3-Day Preview: $45.00 **Purchase Price $550.00**

ORDER #V-2001 **SUPERVISOR IN TRANSITION** - No job is going to change more than that of the first-line supervisor as organizations move forward to improve employee participation, quality, productivity, morale, continuous improvement, etc. This video will help your supervisors gain an understanding of why things *must* change and what they can do to facilitate change in themselves and others. Time: 27 minutes
3-Day Preview: $45.00 **Purchase Price $550.00**

ORDER #V-10 **REDESIGNING A WORKPLACE FOR SELF-REGULATION** - A unionized chemical manufacturing plant that has redesigned its entire operation.
In the last 10 years, the Rohm & Haas Chemical Plant in Louisville, Kentucky and its two unions have cooperated and redesigned 18 work units for self-management. This video documents their journey and the dramatic improvements in quality, customer satisfaction and productivity that have come from employee involvement and self-management. See how they did it step-by-step. Time: 34 minutes. Available in Spanish.
1-Week Preview $45.00 **Purchase Price $495.00**
Prices Subject to Change.

Call To Preview *Complete* Tape
914-528-0888 *We Ship Same Day!*
*We add tapes constantly—Call for info on new releases!

We Would Like To Hear From You:

Call or write to us to let us know how you used this book:

1. What information did you find particularly helpful?

2. What, if anything, would you like to see included in future reprints?

3. What ideas on SDWTs have you formed from your experience that might be useful to other people?

4. What books, articles, other resources have you found helpful?

5. Would you be available to call or visit as a resource?

6. Would you like the names of other people you could use as a resource?

Call (914) 528-0888, or Fax (914) 528-8889, or write to MW Corporation, 3150 Lexington Avenue, Mohegan Lake, New York 10547. Ask for Ann or Bob Harper.

Notes

Notes

Notes